Ask the Right Questions; Get the Right Job

Ask the Right Questions; Get the Right Job

Navigating the Job Interview to Take Control of Your Career

Edward Barr

BUSINESS EXPERT PRESS
Leader in applied, concise business books

Ask the Right Questions; Get the Right Job:
Navigating the Job Interview to Take Control of Your Career

Copyright © Business Expert Press, LLC, 2021.

Cover design by Charlene Kronstedt

Interior design by Exeter Premedia Services Private Ltd., Chennai, India

First published in 2021 by
Business Expert Press, LLC
222 East 46th Street, New York, NY 10017
www.businessexpertpress.com

ISBN-13: 978-1-63742-105-5 (paperback)
ISBN-13: 978-1-63742-106-2 (e-book)

Business Expert Press Business Career Development
Collection

Collection ISSN: 2642-2123 (print)
Collection ISSN: 2642-2131 (electronic)

First edition: 2021

10 9 8 7 6 5 4 3 2 1

Description

Too often people go to interviews prepared only to answer questions. They study the tough questions for days hoping to give the right responses on D-Day. These same people treat the interview as a cross examination; they see themselves on trial, under the spotlight, deer in the headlights. People who are being interviewed need another attitude, an attitude that says, "I'm here to interview you, to see if I want to bring my talents and experiences to your organization." Most people don't know how to do this. However, if armed with a few questions, they can even the playing field and engage in a useful conversation with their hosts.

This book provides a set of questions that are appropriate for any job candidate to ask and allows candidates to participate in a dialogue, a conversation. Experience suggests that only a handful of questions are necessary in most interviews. Review all of the questions. Choose the ones that you believe provide you with the information you need. Learn to interview the interviewer!

Keywords

interview; candidate; preparation; questions; Internet; ask; mission; values; vision; strengths; competencies; rituals; orientation; salary; automation; face-to-face; telephone; virtual

Contents

Foreword

This is advice that I wish I had had before I went blindly into my first interview—and the several after that as well! In the early years of a career, one's perspective simply isn't broad enough to know what questions to ask. At least new grads have an excuse—I must say that, in my experience, many people well into their careers don't know what to ask either! So, in either case, this book will be a very useful tool.

From a company's point of view, a candidate who asked these questions would be like a breath of fresh air. Skill fit is necessary but not sufficient; the rest of identifying the right candidate is all about the fit with the company. A bad hire (where the employee's values and needs don't match what the company has to offer) is a *lose–lose* situation for the company and the employee. Your questions give the candidate an opportunity to differentiate himself or herself from the other candidates, which is extremely helpful to the interviewer.

Ellen Johnston
Former Senior Director, Talent Management
Varian Medical Systems, Palo Alto

Acknowledgments

For my wife, Holly Welty-Barr, who makes the good things in my life possible and who lent me unending support and invaluable advice in writing this book. Also, to Scott Isenberg who believed in this book, and Vilma Barr, an outstanding editor who reviewed the book and made suggestions for its improvement. I thank you.

Introduction

In my 35 years of experience in management and education, I have interviewed many prospective employees and counseled many students preparing for job interviews. Almost universally, I have found both groups, candidates and students, unprepared for their interviews. I don't mean to say that they weren't dressed well, or weren't eager and ready to answer the questions to be posed to them. Most were. They were, as young people can be, enthusiastic and effervescing with optimism and expectation. However, most of them considered the interview a one-sided affair where the potential employer and the employer's representative have all the power—to interrogate, accept, or dismiss them.

Teaching in the Master of Science in Computational Finance program and the Heinz College of Public Policy and Management at Carnegie Mellon University, I have counseled scores of students from all over the world. I have encouraged them to consider their interview and prospective employment differently, that is, as a partnership, a marriage in the truest sense, a commitment of their time, talent, and energies—at a minimum a mutual exchange. And, as a former Chief Marketing Officer at a Carnegie Mellon University for-profit company, and as Vice President of Marketing at a large university health system's medical practice division (and Director of Corporate Communications at a successful for-profit television production company), I interviewed and hired for a variety of staff positions. In addition, I chose outside vendors to meet certain marketing needs for the organization.

I use my years of experience to try to convince my Carnegie Mellon students and others who come to me for advice to approach an interview on equal terms with their potential employers. After all, as prospective employees, they bring with them the skills, talents, and creativity to enrich (in the fullest meaning of the word) the workplace of their employers. Why should they not view the interview as an equal exchange, a true dialogue?

A student visited me lamenting his recent performance in interviews. He kept saying, "I really wanted them to choose me." I stopped him. "But, did you really want to work for them? How could you make that decision when your whole mindset focused on the employer choosing you? A better mindset, one that allows for a more confident presentation of you as the candidate, would have been to be thinking, 'Do I want to work for them?' That would encourage you to ask more questions and engage the interviewer."

With that predisposition, candidates enter the job interview ready to learn as much about the employer as the employer wishes to learn about them. They do this by preparing, if not in writing, at least in their minds, a set of questions the prospective employer must answer. These questions vary from the global (what is this organization's mission) to the specific (are employees encouraged to use personal time).

I am, of course, anxious to tell my student friends, and some of the others who find their way to me, others who have no job or wish to change jobs, that they must maintain respect, perspective, and decorum, that is, they must not be arrogant about this questioning. This applies to face-to-face interviewing as well as to virtual interviewing, which has become very popular, both with humans and machines. After all, the prospective employer does have the ultimate power.

I have found that dialogue in an interview helps to reveal the most information about not only the candidate, but also the prospective employer. This dialogue helps a potentially deadly one-hour session become more interesting, enjoyable, and productive. And, most importantly, it gives the job candidate more of the kind of useful information he or she definitely needs to make the right decision about accepting a position.

Does it guarantee a perfect match between candidate and employer? No, it does not. NO set of questions will. Does asking these questions replace other intelligence-gathering activities? No, it does not. Candidates must use the Internet, published reports, contacts within the organization, competitors, and any other source they can find to learn more about the organization whose company they hope to keep.

Ask the questions pertinent to you from the following pages, and you will see how well the organization has prepared, or ingrained in, your interviewer the kind of information that should be there (and his or her interpretation of that information).

In many ways, a job interview is an unnatural act. Two people sit in front of each other, face-to-face or on a virtual platform, and pretend, both portraying themselves in the very best light and ignoring any frailties. When you ask questions, you can begin to break that façade and both of you benefit. Add these questions to your repertoire, along with enthusiasm, a good cover letter and resume, and a genuine interest in the company and its representatives, to win yourself a great job!

Getting the Interview

Before you can prepare for the interview, you must get the interview. Many books have been written about how to get an interview. I will survey a few of the tactics here.

Networking

Nothing, yes, nothing beats networking for learning about jobs and getting the all-important information that leads to an interview. You must use your contacts and keep them informed of your status and desires. They know where the jobs are and who the gatekeepers are.

A recent Jobvite survey stated that 60 percent of employers' best candidates are found through referrals. It also showed that 73 percent of recruiters have hired a candidate through social media. And, 93 percent of recruiters review a candidate's social profile before making a decision[1].

According to Indeed.com,

Networking for a job requires strategic thinking and developing skills that help you connect with others. By networking efficiently, you can guarantee that the effort you put into cultivating these relationships is worth your time and the time of your colleagues.

Here are a few tips to consider when networking for your next job:

1. Get face-to-face
2. Offer help
3. Fight your fear
4. Be patient and make time
5. Focus on the relationship, not your resume
6. Use social networks and online resources
7. Follow up.[2]

---

[1] https://ziprecruiter.com/blog/how-networking-can-help-you-get-your-next-job/
[2] https://indeed.com/career-advice/finding-a-job/how-to-network-for-a-job

I suggest that the most important item on that list is *offer help*. Most of my LinkedIn connections work in the for-profit space, but nearly all of them volunteer with not-for-profit agencies. One way to help them is to volunteer to help as they help their chosen agency.

Number six on that list means that you must become a content expert of some kind. Take a stand on issues (this relates to #3, *fight your fear*). Write about the things that bother you or thrill you. Post articles from others. Repost. Have a presence.

LinkedIn

The Jobvite survey mentioned social media. That includes LinkedIn, of course. By now, everyone should know about LinkedIn and have a presence there. That means a great head shot and headline.

Career Sidekick offers some good advice about how to use LinkedIn[3]. Most importantly, it advises candidates to write their accomplishments as measurable outcomes and results. Describe your skills in a way that allows a diverse group of employers to immediately see the applicability of you skills to their company. Have a friend review your information for appeal, accuracy, and readability.

Also, get your peers and colleagues to write recommendations for you on your LinkedIn page. I have been asked many times to recommend former colleagues and students and have never once refused. In fact, I have written unsolicited recommendations for people because I thought they deserved the praise.

Be enthusiastic, above all. This word means *with spirit* or *with god*. It comes from the old Greek, *en theos*. We may think of enthusiasm as only being expressed verbally, but using strong descriptive language adds energy to your LinkedIn page. We love people with energy and high spirit. We are attracted to them and want to be around them. Show the world your energy.

---

[3] https://careersidekick.com/use-linkedin-to-find-job/

All-Applicable Social Media

Social media has changed the world. Nearly four billion people use social media[4]. Of course, lots of social media includes photos and videos of cats, dogs, memes, and political views.

But, it can do wonders for someone searching for a job. Recruiters regularly check out social media. SHRM has said that 84 percent of companies are using social media for hiring[5].

A Harris poll said that employers check the social media profiles of candidates, and 57 percent are less likely to interview a candidate with no online presence, and 54 percent failing to hire a candidate because of the candidate's social media profiles[6].

Add to that the fact that 30 percent of employers have human resource (HR) personnel dedicated to social recruiting[7].

You gotta use social media.

Alumni

If you are a high-school graduate or a college graduate, you have connections, even if they're not your best friends. Use your former schools to find alumni who are working in industries that you wish to join. Write to these people. Introduce yourself and find some connection. Maybe you both were once members of the same sorority but years apart. Maybe you both played baseball or played in the band. Ask for their help in acquiring information or introductions. They are usually happy to help

---

[4] https://blog.hootsuite.com/simon-kemp-social-media/

[5] https://shrm.org/resourcesandtools/hr-topics/talent-acquisition/pages/using-social-media-find-passive-candidates.aspx#:~:text=The%20SHRM%20survey%20%E2%80%9CUsing%20Social,percent%20planning%20to%20use%20it

[6] http://press.careerbuilder.com/2018-08-09-More-Than-Half-of-Employers-Have-Found-Content-on-Social-Media-That-Caused-Them-NOT-to-Hire-a-Candidate-According-to-Recent-CareerBuilder-Survey

[7] http://press.careerbuilder.com/2017-06-15-Number-of-Employers-Using-Social-Media-to-Screen-Candidates-at-All-Time-High-Finds-Latest-Career-Builder-Study

xx GETTING THE INTERVIEW

because they have been in your situation and know what a little help can do. Connect to former teachers, to career offices, and certainly to alumni offices for the names and addresses of former students.

College Honor Societies

National honor societies, like sororities and fraternities, have extensive membership rolls. If you belonged to any one of these organizations, use them to make connections to the people who can help you.

Professional Organizations

Just about every profession has related professional organizations, local, state, and national (and some international), you can use your membership in these organizations to connect to the kind of people who can help in your job search. Many of these organizations have job boards anyway where they post positions. Use these professional organizations to open your connections.

Family, Friends, Associates

This could be the lowest-hanging fruit. Get the word out to your family, friends, colleagues, and neighbors, anyone who you believe might be able to help you. Sometimes, knowledge of jobs comes from the most unlikely of sources.

News Stories

Read the news every day and look for information about the expected growth of companies, their expected acquisitions. Look at announcements of promotions and changes in jobs. Learn where the action is, as well as the opportunities.

Employers Want These Kinds of Employees

I have worked on the for-profit side and the not-for-profit side at startups and at old and established organizations, and I have found that employers are all looking for the same kinds of people:

- Employees who can think strategically
- Employees who are self-motivated
- Employees who will do more than their job description mandates
- Employees who are mature
- Employees who are ethical
- Employees who can play well with others

Strategic Thinking

Most companies furnish new employees with a job description and set of goals, as well as some general supervision. But, often, employees find themselves in situations that require strategic thinking, outside their normal day-to-day experience. In these situations, employees must take actions based in an organization's mission and values as well as its vision and strategic plan. In other words, employees are required to make wise decisions when the answers don't immediately reveal themselves. We like to think that we can hire people who can deal with these unexpected situations and make prudent decisions. Often, recruiters ask behavioral questions to try to tease out the candidate's ability to think.

Self-Motivation

I would rather hire someone I had to chase than someone I had to jump-start every day. I'd rather hire someone who made mistakes while trying many things, than someone who did very little and made absolutely no mistakes. I'd rather hire someone to whom I handed a job description and set of goals and said, "OK, go to it!" This means I'd like to hire someone whom I have carefully vetted as intelligent and eager, someone who can grow beyond the job, and become all that she promises to be. I'm not unhappy with someone who has the spotlight and believes that all managers should be transparent, that all managers should guide and teach, not manage, in the negative sense of the word. As a result, I believe the best *managers* are those who find and hire self-motivated people and give them plenty of room to experiment and grow.

Desire to Grow

I have always found that there is more work in every organization than there are people willing to do it. Therefore, I have looked for employees who can demonstrate, through behavioral questions and interview conversations, that they have looked for and volunteered to do the extra work that exists in any organization. These people are not tied to a job description; they don't say, "Sorry, that's not my responsibility." This is especially true for customer-facing positions.

Maturity

This quality is hard to gauge. Again, I will ask a series of behavioral questions designed to determine if a person has the maturity to make wise decisions. These questions are no secret and are used often: "Tell me about a time when you had to redo your work. Tell me about a time when your work was criticized. Tell me about a time you disagreed with your boss."

Ethics

Businesses are becoming more and more transparent. The public demands to know how companies are operating. They want to know a company's ethics. Companies want to know that the people they employ will have positive, strong ethics. Again, recruiters will likely use behavioral questions to tease out the ethics of the people sitting before them in an interview.

These questions are also common: "Tell me about a time when you were asked to do something you felt was unethical. If you never had that happen, what would you do if someone offered you a free trip to Europe if you recommended their product for purchase by your company?"

Teamwork

These days, most employees work in self-directed teams. They must clearly define their positions and responsibilities and make a commitment, they must agree to be open to constructive feedback and accept some conflict, they must agree on timeframes, and above all, they must develop complete trust in each other. Recruiters use behavioral questions to tease out answers here, also. Are you comfortable working with others, or did you feel more comfortable working alone?

Why Should You Ask Questions?

I have occasionally begun interviews in this way:

ME: Thank you for coming today. We are interviewing only the best candidates who responded to our posting on LinkedIn and yours was one of the best. We have a great team in our department, and we hire only after careful consideration. I have created an agenda for our meeting today (I hand the applicant a copy of it). Take a look at this; it includes some of the questions I would like us to discuss. Don't feel that you have to memorize these, or that there are any perfect answers. (Pause) Are there any items you'd like to add (if no, I move on)? All right. You will note that my first question asks if you have any questions about this position.

CANDIDATE: (Some candidates are befuddled and reply in the negative. The rare candidate will begin with a powerful and important question, such as: Tell me a little about your team. Or, what makes your team gel? Or, what is your management style? Or, what are your primary goals for this year? More on this later when we discuss mock interviews.

Most interviews do not begin this way, as far as I know. But, because I have been a marketing person for most of my career, I'm interested in the customer point of view, and I have always perceived the job candidate as my customer. If we have a great interview, a true conversation, and I don't hire that person, I hope to leave her or him feeling good about the company and anxious to reapply, should another vacancy arise. And, if we come to terms on employment, I have created a positive impression for this person to begin working in our team.

In any event, you must prepare to ask questions for the following reasons:

- Ask questions to show your interest in the position and the company

- Show that you are an assertive person, not aggressive, but assertive
- Show the depth of your intelligence
- Show your energy

Speaking of energy, I have told students to begin by saying, "I am so excited to be here and I welcome this opportunity." This sets the stage for a positive experience by priming both candidate and employer. When you say this with conviction and energy, you also set the stage for asking questions.

Stupid Questions

There are questions that inspire conversation and those that don't. Don't ask the following questions.

Stupid Question 1

Questions that begin with *when*, *where*, and *who*?

If you ask someone a question that begins with *when*, you will initiate a one-word answer. The same holds true for *where* and *who* questions. But, if you ask a *why* or a *how* or a *what* question, you will initiate a fuller response. If you ask, does your company offer paternity leave, you will create a one-word response. Instead, you might ask, "How does your company support parents who have children?" You will likely inspire an answer that's something like this: "We understand the needs of our employees and like to think of ourselves as family-friendly. As such, we offer six weeks of leave for women who have given birth and six weeks for their partners. To us, work-life balance is not just important, it's critical."

Stupid Question 2

Questions that are too much focused on you.

We are all motivated by self-interest; that's a fact. It helps keep us alive. But, too much focus on your needs suggests that you are not interested enough in the needs of the company with whom you are interviewing. Don't ask questions about tuition benefits, relocation expenses, support for student loans, and so forth. Save those for the negotiation stage, after you have been offered the position. Keep your focus on what the company needs and how you can fulfill their needs. Tell stories about how you have satisfied similar needs in another setting.

Stupid Question 3

Questions that anyone would already know.

If you interview at Apple, and you ask the recruiter "Who founded Apple?," you will look like the world's biggest fool. The same goes for any facts that are easily able to be found on a company's website. That said, you can ask your interviewer if she or he knows the company mission and values. Or, you can ask how the employees are living the mission/values/vision and so forth. Employees who are fully invested in their place of work know these things and are proud of them. This should be especially true for recruiters. But, remember to ask these questions with the right tone and attitude. If you ask with hostility, you will be perceived as hostile.

Stupid Question 4

Antagonistic questions.

There are ways to pose questions. For example, if you ask, "Is it true that your CEO was just accused of having an affair with her secretary?," you are asking for an argument. You are better off phrasing a question such as that one like this: "Are there any activities on-going in the company that jeopardize its ability to continue to function well in the market?" The same rule should apply to any questions that touch on politics, such as, "Do you think it's wise for your company to be expanding into China?" You are better off asking a question such as, "What are the company's plans for growth this year?"

Stupid Question 5

Questions that are just plain stupid.

If you ask the recruiter these questions, you will not likely be hired:

- Do you offer mental health benefits?
- Do people have to work more than 40 hours/week?
- Do I, or does the company, get the frequent flier miles when I travel?

- How long do I have to work before I accrue vacation?
- Will you be doing a credit check?
- Does a misdemeanor conviction rule out a candidate?
- Do you hire relatives?
- Can you give me examples of (Indians, Pakistanis, Saudis, or any other ethnic group) who work here?
- And, similar stupid questions!

The Right Questions

Yes, there are stupid questions to ask, but the stupidest question is the one you don't ask. As we've been saying, you demonstrate your interest, your enthusiasm, and your intelligence when you engage in a conversation with a recruiter. Otherwise, you sit there like a lamppost or, worse yet, a dartboard, either motionless or inert or catching the darts as they are tossed at you. So, here again is the list that we will explore in the coming pages. Review them and learn how to use them to make your next interview an interactive and successful one.

1. What is the corporate mission?
2. What are the corporate values?
3. What is the corporate culture?
4. What is the organization's vision?
5. Does the organization have a strategic plan?
6. What are the organization's strengths?
7. What are the areas where the organization can improve?
8. What is the organization's financial projection for the coming year?
9. What are the company's core competencies?
10. Does the company have rituals?
11. What communication techniques does the organization use with employees?
12. Does the company value diversity?
13. What is the organization's board makeup and involvement?
14. Does the company have programs to develop and promote minorities?
15. How is the organization positioned in the market?
16. How do you define the organization's market and share of market?
17. Who are the company's main competitors?
18. Has the organization ever faced a crisis? What was the crisis, and how did the company respond?
19. How do problems get resolved in the organization?

20. Is there a union at the organization?
21. What do the workspaces look like in the company?
22. How would you describe the company environment?
23. Is there a corporate dress code?
24. Who are the corporate heroes/heroines? What are the corporate myths?
25. What characteristics does the model employee of the company possess?
26. What skills are valued most?
27. How would you describe the successful manager in the company?
28. Does the organization have a *recognition-rich* environment?
29. What is the organization's retention rate?
30. What opportunities exist for training and staff development?
31. Does the organization have profit sharing, gain sharing, an ESOP?
32. How are customer relations handled?
33. Does the organization support any cause?
34. How flexible is the company?
35. Is the organization parent-friendly?
36. Does the company provide a new employee orientation?
37. Does the organization require employees to write goals?
38. How are employees evaluated?
39. Does a job description exist for this position?
40. What is the typical day and workload like for this position?
41. Have there been any lay-offs recently?
42. What techniques does the company use to increase morale?
43. How long have you been with the company?
44. How many people are you interviewing for this position?
45. What is the process for selection of the final candidate?
46. What is the salary range for this position?
47. What is the benefit package, and is it negotiable?
48. How would you describe, in one word, working at this company?
49. How did I do in this interview?
50. When will I find out that I have been chosen?

PART I

Preparation for the Interview

Do Some Internet Research

Your hard work and patience have paid off! You're finally scheduled for an interview with WayOut.com. You've read 15 books on "How To Prepare For the Interview." You've got the right clothes, conservative but not funereal; you've read all the "Questions You May Be Asked" and memorized the *right* answers, and, you've talked to everyone you know about how to survive this right of passage. You might have even been interviewed before or had a *mock interview*. Now it's time to think of the questions you're going to ask at the interview.

You are an ethical, honest human being who wants to work for a company committed to the same virtues. You have studied the *right questions* and want to know about mission, values, and corporate responsibility.

You can learn the mission, values, and strategic direction of a company simply by visiting their website. Take a look at Dell.com, for instance[1]. Click on "About Dell" and you will find "Careers," "Newsroom," "Investors," and "Social Impact." Scroll down and you'll also find, "Who we are," "Our brands," "Leadership," and "Sponsorships." Open "Who we are" and scroll down to "Powering human progress: developing technology to transform lives" and the "Dell Technologies Code of Conduct." Here you will find some important things to know about the company you may wish to join.

---

[1] https://dell.com/en-us

If you Google the founder, you will see that Michael Dell started the company in 1984 with the uncommon idea of selling custom-built computers directly to the customer. Dell Technologies defines itself as having used *the power of direct to customers* to provide customers with superb value; high-quality, relevant technology; customized systems; superior service and support; and products and services that are easy to buy and use.

When you click on "Commitment," you'll find Michael Dell saying: "Integrity matters. It matters to our customers, partners, colleagues and communities. And, it matters greatly to me." As a result, the company says that it will "…avoid conflicts of interests…engage in charitable contributions and activities…and make values-based decisions," among other things. It then gives a half dozen or so e-mail addresses where ethics violations can be reported.

When you're looking for a place to spend at least 40 hours a week of your life, look for this information, among other things:

- Mission
- Values
- Social responsibility
- Diversity
- Community involvement

Questions that you can find answered on the Internet (or in available company publications, such as the annual report)
If you persevere with your search, you can find just about anything on the Internet, but you should be able to find answers to these important questions readily.

1. What is the corporate mission?
2. What are the corporate values?
13. What is the organization's board makeup and involvement?
15. How is the organization positioned in the market?
16. How do you define the organization's market and share of market?
17. Who are the company's main competitors?

Question to Ask for-Profits
Questions to Ask Not-for-Profits (Nonprofits)

Obviously, the motives of for-profits and not-for-profits (nonprofits) differ around the word "profit." Both are typically responsible to a board, and both must be well managed and maintained financially, but only one is responsible to shareholders to create a financial return for shareholder investment, although the situation is shifting somewhat with for-profits developing community-minded instincts. (Not-for-profits and nonprofits differ slightly but mostly around the bottom line; nonprofits typically show a zero balance at the end of their reporting year.)

What to Ask at a Not-for-Profit (Nonprofit) Interview

Not-for-profit organizations (or nonprofits) usually have a specific mission and target audience. Think of the American Heart Association, the American Cancer Society, the Society for the Prevention of Cruelty to Animals, the World Health Organization, Center for Disease Control, and many, many other governmental, healthcare, special interest, and public policy-centered groups.

Mission Versus Margin

Most not-for-profits live by their mission. It's not that they don't care about the margin; it's not their very first priority. A health care organization in my city yearly brags of a bottom line in the billions of dollars; its CEO is paid several million dollars a year in salary. Many say that they act more like a for-profit. They may, indeed, but they return none of their equity to any shareholders. They probably advertise as much as any for-profit organization in this state, but, again, they reinvest most of their money in the organization. They don't pay dividends and have no shareholders.

If you interview with a company like that, ask them the following questions and remember you are asking them to see if the mission and values are ingrained and alive with the employees, or just hot air spouted on their website and other promotional materials:

1. What is the corporate mission?
2. What are the corporate values?
3. What is the corporate culture?
4. What is the organization's vision?
5. Does the organization have a strategic plan?
6. What are the organization's strengths?
7. What are the areas where the organization can improve?
8. What is the organization's financial projection for the coming year?

Most not-for-profits depend on the donations of contributors to meet their expanses. Some depend on the government or agencies like the United Way. Knowing this, you should ask these kinds of questions: "How dependable is your donor base? Will the government support continue into the next year? If your donations might diminish, do you have plans to make up for the shortfall?"

If you are interviewing at a for-profit, many of the same questions apply, but some are different.

What to Ask at a For-Profit Interview

For-profit companies have been gradually changing, but they still focus on shareholder return to the exclusion of the environment, social issues and governance. In fact, they seem to pay attention to these only in so far as they can make a better profit by doing so. Be that as it may, you should ask the following kinds of questions at an interview with a for-profit company.

3. What is the corporate culture?
4. What is the organization's vision?
5. Does the organization have a strategic plan?
6. What are the organization's strengths?
7. What are the areas where the organization can improve?
8. What is the organization's financial projection for the coming year?
9. What are the company's core competencies?

Fit the Questions Smoothly
Into the Interview

Certainly, any of the questions can be fit in the context of the interview. For example, if someone asks, "What has been your experience managing a budget?" And, I would hope an interviewer would ask a potential manager that question. Then, you can cite your experience and insert your question about the financial status of the company.

NOTE: You should act professionally at the interview. You should act interested, confident, mature, and serious. You are not at the interview to establish an antagonistic relationship. You do that and you have better-than-average chances of being passed over for the job. No one likes to interview disrespectful or derisive candidates.

Suppose you are asked the techniques you use to resolve conflict. Again, I would hope as a potential manager you would be asked that question. If you are asked, you have a perfect, and legitimate, opportunity to ask questions about how the company communicates with its various constituencies, handles crises, and recognizes people.

I suggest you pose these questions in a subtle or straightforward manner, whatever your personality. This means you should be yourself. Don't interview and pretend to be someone you're not. If you get the job based on a false persona, you will eventually revert to your "real" self and either you and/or your new employer may become very dissatisfied.

If a potential employer is intimidated that you ask some legitimate questions, you should seriously consider whether you want to work there. Remember, don't take a job simply to have a job. It's the worst thing you can do. You will find the right job. Persevere. Even in the Great Depression, 70 percent of the workforce had jobs.

Prioritize Your Questions

What happens if you don't have time or chance to ask several questions? What should you consider the most important question?

The answer to this certainly depends on your interview context and the personality of the interviewer. That said, I believe the most important questions have to do with your actual job duties and the evaluation of your performance. Therefore, if you can ask only one question (or one group of questions), I advise you to ask, "Does the organization require employees to write goals? How are employees evaluated?"

Never accept a job without a clear definition of your duties. Never stay in a job where you have no specific, measurable, and negotiated goals to perform and with which to be measured by.

Too many employers and their supervisors fail to use specific measurable goals and work plans and fall victim to the "I like him/her. Let's give her/him a raise. She/he's doing a nice job." That's fine, as long as your boss likes you. However, if your relationship with your boss becomes challenging, with measurable goals and evaluations, you cannot be denied a raise if you meet them. In a worst-case scenario, you cannot be fired for arbitrary reasons. Management must demonstrate that you failed to meet goals that you both agreed upon. In either scenario, having measurable goals to measure your performance against is important to your long- and short-term success in a job.

Ask the Most Important Questions

5. Does the organization have a strategic plan?
8. What is the organization's financial projection for the coming year?
25. What characteristics does the model employee of the company possess?
26. What skills are valued most?
30. What opportunities exist for training and staff development?
37. Does the organization require employees to write goals?
38. How are employees evaluated?
39. Does a job description exist for this position?
44. How many people are you interviewing for this position?
45. What is the process for selection of the final candidate?
49. How did I do in this interview?
50. When will I find out that I have been chosen?

Ask the HR Representative These Questions

Human resource (HR) people know a lot about company policies, employee relations, hiring and firing, and benefits as well as specific job responsibilities. They have formulas for interviewing. They've taken courses that tell them how to identify good and bad characteristics. They can stereotype you right out of a good job. However, most job interviews begin with HR, and most organizations depend upon them to screen out inappropriate candidates.

You must be very careful interviewing with HR people. You can't show up on either end of the scale, either too aggressive or too passive. You must perform in the middle for them. By all means, ask them questions. They like engaged people. And, they like the big, broad questions: "Does the company value diversity?" They like that question because they are charged, largely, for creating and maintaining diversity.

You might ask the HR people about union activity. I say *might* because they are often anti-union, as they are charged with dealing with grievances and negotiating salaries and benefits, areas of concern to unions. Tread cautiously with this one.

You can ask HR people about retention rates, profit sharing, training and development, even recognition programs. They'll love it! And, speaking of salaries and benefits, HR people are consumed with salary and benefit knowledge. Ask about the 501 c (3). They'll love you! Questions related to benefits and dress codes are specific to HR; these questions should not be asked during interviews with managers, they waste time and managers are often unsure of the answers.

Here is a list of questions from which you can choose if you are interviewed in the company HR department.

12. Does the company value diversity?
14. Does the company have programs to develop and promote minorities?
20. Is there a union at the organization?
21. What do the workspaces look like in the company?
22. How would you describe the company environment?
23. Is there a corporate dress code?
28. Does the organization have a "Recognition-Rich" environment?
29. What is the organization's retention rate?
30. What opportunities exist for training and staff development?
31. Does the organization have profit sharing, gain sharing, an ESOP?

35. Is the organization parent-friendly?

36. Does the company provide a new employee orientation?

37. Does the organization require employees to write goals?

38. How are employees evaluated?

39. Does a job description exist for this position?

41. Have there been any lay-offs recently?

42. What techniques does the company use to increase morale?

46. What is the salary range for this position?

47. What is the benefit package, and is it negotiable?

PART II

The Right Questions

SECTION 1

Ask About the Company

Question 1

What Is the Corporate Mission?

Yes, mission and values come and go, into and out of favor. But, really, what is more important about an organization than what it stands for, what it values, and why it exists? You will want to ask about the organization's profitability. You will want to ask about its many operating procedures, but if you don't know what makes it tick, what drives it onward, what it strives to become, you will not know the company.

Author and leadership guru, Simon Sinek has encouraged organizations and their leaders to "Start With Why[1]." He has said that people don't buy what a company does, but why it does it. That why is the mission. It's what you've been *sent* to do (the world mission comes from a Latin root for sending).

I worked in the Pittsburgh Mercy Health System, parent of the first Mercy Hospital in the world, Mercy Hospital of Pittsburgh. For over 150 years, the hospital was led by a Sister of Mercy. The Sister chief executive officer (CEO) I worked for made the mission and values living things. I might have had them branded on my arm; I knew them so well, from iteration and practice. I, and most of my colleagues, knew well what Mercy stood for. It stood for creating a healthy community—creating wellness, eliminating disease, physical, mental, or systemic.

---

[1] https://amazon.com/Start-Why-Leaders-Inspire-Everyone/dp/1591846447/ref=sr_1_3?crid=MVZIL0VKNW35&dchild=1&keywords=simon+sinek&qid=1609865233&s=books&sprefix=simon+%2Caps%2C172&sr=1-3

You should be able to find a company's mission statement on its website, if it has one. Or, you should be able to find it in its published documents—the annual report, the quarterly reports, the sales literature, or the recruiting materials.

Look at these documents. If you can't find the mission or mission language, ask the question in the interview. You may have to ask obliquely, that is, you may have to ask the question indirectly. You might say, "Why is this company doing business?" If a for-profit says, "To make a profit," they will answer honestly, but you might also expect them to add, "and to create and maintain satisfied customers" or even "to make the world a better place." Regardless of how you ask, however, find the answer.

And, speaking of knowing the company, asking about the mission and values will present a good opportunity for you to find out what your interviewer knows about the company he or she represents. (It will show you how the organization's leaders keep the mission alive and apparent in their employees.)

Make this one your first question! Search the Internet and the company's published documents for the words of the mission.

Companion Questions to This One
    2. What are the corporate values?
    3. What is the corporate culture?
    4. What is the organization's vision?

Question 2

What Are the Corporate Values?

When I worked at the Pittsburgh Mercy Health System (which has since become part of the University of Pittsburgh Medical Center), the six corporate values were easy to find. They were published on almost all of our internal communications. I knew them well and still remember them—compassion, collaboration, community, stewardship, excellence, and human dignity. We joked that the first letters of each value spelled "SHE C's," a reference, of course, to the top Sister of Mercy.

And, she did see, as well she should have! Each of these values was defined, and each employee of Mercy, including the CEO, was expected to live the value at work. Many times, I used our value of collaboration to keep others, less imbued with the values, from treating employees of lesser rank in the organization disrespectfully. I merely called the person, repeated the incident, and reminded them of the corporate values. They often apologized, recognizing their mistake.

And, make no mistake, not all employees will live each value. Nonetheless, because the value is in place, we all at least strived to live by it. And, so should those in the company where you may be offered employment.

Will your interviewers know the corporate values as I knew Mercy's? It's hard to say. Maybe the *hard core* people will. You know, they're the ones who have the company logo tattooed somewhere on their person, the *gung-ho* types.

As with the corporate mission, you may be able to find the corporate values listed on the website. For instance, check your favorite company's site. Do they invest ethically with an eye toward environmental, social, and governance (ESG; the so-called *sustainable investing*)? Are they interested in global issues, such as climate change? Do they invest in the companies that use renewable resources? Are they an enlightened company? Do they live their values? You judge! If you're interviewing there, ask the person who interviews you. Remember, you're hiring them, just as they are hiring you!

One last comment on values. We all had to write goals at Mercy, and our goals required that we include a "values goal." From year to year, I typically wrote my values goal like this: "To train 30 tutors to work with the illiterate in Pittsburgh literacy programs over the 12 month period." That was a measurable goal and brought the values to life.

Companion Questions to This One
1. What is the corporate mission?
3. What is the corporate culture?
4. What is the organization's vision?

Question 3

What Is the Corporate Culture?

Every organization has a culture, or a personality, if you prefer.

I once worked as Director of Corporate Communications at a television production company. We created television commercials, corporate video, sports programming, and duplication and distribution of television programming. We interacted with advertising agencies, network producers, and public relations (PR) people, among others.

Our CEO and Executive Vice President (VP), who founded the firm, came from one of what was then called *The Big Eight* accounting firms. They wore conservative suits and ties every day (and so did I). And, they were very conservative in all aspects of their lives. Nonetheless, even though they were conservative business types, they knew that to succeed in the television production business, the firm needed not only solid fiscal grounding but lots of creativity, as well. Hence, they encouraged and fostered creativity.

The culture of that firm was what I would call *Adolescent*. It had the personality of Adam Sandler. The directors, camera operators, lighting and sound experts all dressed in the latest and most outlandish tee shirts and jeans. Anyone who walked onto a set in a suit was automatically suspect and shunned. This was a firm not only in its teenage years in actual years of operation but also in its culture. They produced fine work and were valued by the ad agencies, television networks, and corporations we did work for, and, it was, in part, because of the freewheeling energy of the creative types.

On the other extreme, the culture at Mercy was very maternal and spiritual, as befitting a health care organization founded and presided over by a religious order of women, most of whom wore drab, ordinary clothing and no makeup. (Interestingly, after I became Director of Corporate Communications at Mercy and we needed to produce television commercials, we used two men from the other firm, and they produced award-winning video communications for us.)

You can learn a little about the culture by looking at the organization's website and publications. How do the employees dress? Does it use lively graphics? Does it use informal language? Does it use pinstripes or gothic type? You can certainly learn the culture by visiting the company, looking around, and asking employees. Yes, visit the company and interview some of the workers. Why not? Hey, "It's a free country!"

Companion Questions to This One
1. What is the corporate mission?
2. What are the corporate values?
4. What is the organization's vision?

Question 4

What Is the Organization's Vision?

Heraclitus, a famous Greek philosopher, said, "Everything changes." This certainly applies to organizations. Every organization must change or die. No organization can remain the same in the midst of a continuously changing world and marketplace. To direct this change as much as possible, an organization must have a vision of itself for the future.

A vision statement describes where the company aspires to be upon achieving its mission. This statement reveals the *where* of a business. Without a vision statement, a company risks stagnation. Without a vision to attain, they risk losing market position to a competitor that does have a vision, that vision becomes their future. Following are some vision statements from well-known companies to give you a sense of how a vision represents a brand. Take a look at the following vision statements.

Teach for America: One day, all children in this nation will have the opportunity to attain an excellent education.
LinkedIn: Create economic opportunity for every member of the global workforce.
Disney: To entertain, inform and inspire people around the globe through the power of unparalleled storytelling, reflecting the iconic brands, creative minds and innovative technologies that make ours the world's premier entertainment company.
Facebook: Connect with friends and the world around you on Facebook[2].

Do these companies succeed because they have a vision? Do their employees know the vision? Ask the person who interviews you, from whatever company. If that person cannot articulate (or at least paraphrase) the company vision, perhaps one does not exist. Perhaps they have no idea where they're going. Perhaps you don't want to join an organization that's directionless.

---

[2] https://blog.hubspot.com/marketing/inspiring-company-mission-statements

Companion Questions to This One
1. What is the corporate mission?
2. What are the corporate values?
3. What is the corporate mission?

Question 5

Does the Organization Have a Strategic Plan?

Enough has been written about the importance of planning that we need not revisit it here. Needless to say, any organization can benefit from planning. The strategic plan maps out a pathway to achieve the vision for a company. Without it, the company may flounder and fail. The plan itself is of lesser value than the process, and plans constantly change (see Heraclitus). Former heavyweight champion of the world, Mike Tyson, said, "Everybody has a plan till they get punched in the mouth[3]." Obviously, events can occur that require the plan to be revisited and revised using the planning process to map out the company's future and to invest the employees in the company's future.

When you are interviewing, ask if the organization has a strategic plan and a planning process, and, if the company does have a process, ask how it is implemented. This implementation should become obvious to you depending upon your interviewer's response. If he or she is part of a good planning process, he or she will respond quickly and enthusiastically. If the company has no strategic planning or approaches planning in a tedious or haphazard way, the respondent will stumble. A plan not properly implemented or sporadically followed provides not much more guidance than no plan at all. Without a properly formulated and implemented plan, organizations face failure.

For you to know the answer to this question can help you make your decision, if you are offered one, about joining the firm. Then, if you join, you must, in your first week, ask for a copy of the strategic plan. Hey, you will be asked to do your part to achieve the plan's objectives. You need to know what they are.

Companion Questions to This One
  6. What are the organization's strengths?
  7. What are the areas where the organization can improve?
  8. What is the organization's financial situation?
  9. What are the company's core competencies?

---

[3] http://cutandjacked.com/30-Mike-Tyson-Quotes-Photos#!/

Question 6

What Are the Organization's Strengths?

If your interviewer hasn't already done so (and I would hope the interviewer had), he or she should enthusiastically reveal the organization's strengths. This shows pride in the organization, if nothing else. And, if you are treated well at the interview, you walk away as a salesperson for them, knowing what makes them a great company and telling your friends. Hey, they should want everyone to know their strengths.

Any firm that has done strategic planning or market planning has used the strengths, weaknesses, opportunities and threats (SWOT) analysis. They asked themselves to honestly list their strengths, weaknesses, opportunities and threats. So, an institutional list of these characteristics exists somewhere.

You want the list of strengths as perceived by the interviewer, not the official corporate list. If this person cannot generate, out of hand, a list, you may want to rethink your potential relationship with them.

You want to hear them say, "Our people are our strength." Or, "We are financially sound." Or, and perhaps better yet, "Our customers are our greatest strength." Be it as it may, you will want to hear something. You will, of course, be asked that most famous of interview questions, "Tell me your strengths." Every book on interviewing on the market prepares you to be able to respond to this most basic interview question. Why not turn the tables and ask your interviewer that question?

Companion Questions to This One
   5. Does the organization have a strategic plan?
   7. What are the areas where the organization can improve?
   8. What is the organization's financial situation?
   9. What are the company's core competencies?

Question 7

What Are the Areas Where the Organization Can Improve?

Most candidates know they will be asked if they have any weaknesses. Most, by now, also know how to answer, "I work too hard. I just don't know when to stop. I give my all to my employer."

On the other hand, not many interviewers expect to be asked the question. Because they are unprepared, they will likely answer honestly. They will be less likely to have the pat answer such as the one you've memorized for your interviews.

Wouldn't it be good to ask some of the company's current employees what the company's weaknesses are? You might hear, "The benefits are awful," or "This place expects your soul."

Every organization has strengths and weaknesses. It is no cause for shame. In fact, most companies, when they do strategic planning, list many more weaknesses than strengths. It's human nature for us to perceive our weaknesses more than our strengths.

A company aware of its weaknesses makes it able to address them and become that much stronger. Likewise, sharing the good and the bad with its employees makes a company stronger. And, the company that considers employee views and acts on them is a company on the road to invincibility.

Companion Questions to This One
  5. Does the organization have a strategic plan?
  6. What are the organization's strengths?
  8. What is the organization's financial situation?
  9. What are the company's core competencies?

Question 8

What Is the Organization's Financial Projection for the Coming Year?

Even if you investigate thoroughly, you'll always find ENRON whose accounting practices are shady, at best. ENRON hid losses while their executives took millions from the company and its shareholders. You never would have found that looking at the published documents.

One of the key pieces of information you should investigate before interviewing with a company is its financial stability. Annual reports contain much of the important financial data such as net revenue, surpluses after investment income, return on investment, and so forth. So, whatever motivates you, it pays to know the financial position of an organization you consider joining. You then understand some of hurdles you face. I make no claims to financial wizardry; I simply encourage you to gain some understanding of the financial strength of the firm you wish to cast your lot with.

This financial information also tells you how the company spends its money. Does it reinvest in itself? Does it update its equipment? What areas receive the most reinvestment? Companies do not value all divisions equally. An investment company known for commercial banking decided to go into retail banking. They did not invest heavily in it, did not value the employees hired in that area, and eventually closed it, displacing all of the employees. Clearly, anyone looking to join that division would consider working in that division risky, at best, and not a good career choice. You can, of course, learn this information about publicly held companies. They must file their quarterly and annual financial reports with the Securities and Exchange Commission (SEC) and with the people who own their stock. Nonprofits must also file Internal Revenue Service (IRS) reports of their financial wherewithal. With nonprofits, you may legally walk in their doors at any time and ask for a copy of their IRS report. (You may have to pay for the copies and wait a day or two for the report.)

Companion Questions to This One

    5. Does the organization have a strategic plan?

    6. What are the organization's strengths

    7. What are the areas where the organization can improve?

    9. What are the company's core competencies?

Question 9

What Are the Organization's Core Competencies?

If you believe in the Pareto principle[4], and I do, you will agree that 20 percent of a company's output reflects 80 percent of its successes. No company can do everything for everyone.

How many failures can be attributed to the company that "does everything for everyone?" In Pittsburgh, in the 1980s and 1990s, the hospital competition was fierce. However, Children's Hospital cornered pediatric care (and rightfully so). Presbyterian Hospital cornered transplant surgery (they did, after all, retain the world famous transplant surgeon Dr. Thomas Starzl). Magee Women's placed in the top 10 in the United States for women's health matters; Mercy was known as the Catholic hospital, and Allegheny General had the best heart surgery and trauma care (plus the "Life Flight" franchise). They had core competencies in their respective fields. They did other things well, too, but they were best at a few. (See Question 15.)

I've worked at Carnegie Mellon University for many years, and over the years, the university has become well known for teaching computing. It has secondary, niche excellence in theater, computational finance, robotics, public policy, and business. It depends whom you ask.

If you don't already know from your own investigation, ask your interviewer what he or she perceives to be the company's competencies. You may be surprised at the answer.

Knowing the competencies of the company may indicate to you if this is a good career path. For example, a cardiac surgeon interested in transplantation should not seek employment at a community hospital that identifies as such and has no other aspirations. The staff and funding do not exist there to support groundbreaking transplant surgery. Also, be wary of a company that claims competency in many diverse areas but does not appear to have any overlap. If you see this, ask about it. How can company X have competence in areas that have no shared technology or expertise?

---

[4] https://en.wikipedia.org/wiki/Pareto_principle

Companion Questions to This One

    5. Does the organization have a strategic plan?

    6. What are the organization's strengths?

    7. What are the areas where the organization can improve?

    8. What is the organization's financial situation?

Question 10

Does the Company Have Rituals?

Ritualistic behavior is healthy for any organization. At Mercy, we had many rituals, most of them related to spiritual events, like Christmas, Easter, Passover, but others related to Black History Month, Martin Luther King, Jr.'s birthday, and so forth.

At Christmas, the CEO led the decorating of the lobby Christmas tree as well as the singing of carols, all of this in the company of nurses, doctors, technicians, staff, and children from our day care center. Many employees stood in that lobby year after year with their children and celebrated a moment away from their very important work. They celebrated in the presence, and as equals with, the CEO, VPs and management team. This was in keeping, of course, with their stated mission and values.

Other companies have other events. I worked at an organization that took top management to South Carolina each winter for a golf outing. The vast majority of these individuals were men, and the event quickly became known as the "Testosterone Open." By now, the event embraces women equally. Even so, I understand that the bonding was significant, and many work issues were discussed, debated, and resolved.

Some companies participate in the United Way "Day of Caring" and loan their staff to other agencies to help them accomplish objectives, perhaps cleaning or painting, or feeding the homeless. This gives many people a pride in their organization.

Ask your interviewer about corporate rituals. Some may be fun, some serious. Nonetheless, they exist, in every organization, even if it's just celebrating birthdays. If you don't want to use the word *rituals*, ask the interviewer what the staff do to celebrate, or what they do other than work. Ask what holidays are celebrated. Find a way to get at this information. It will tell you about the character of the people and company.

Companion Questions to This One

    11. What communication techniques does the organization use with employees?

Question 11

What Communication Techniques Does the Organization Use With Employees?

As *Cool Hand Luke* in the movie of the same name, Paul Newman mocked the warden of his prison by mimicking his statement, "What we have here is a failure to communicate." We all know what happened to Luke at the end of this great movie; he was shot!

As a person who worked in communication all of my life, I know the value of the practice of communication. I worked in a large corporation with many divisions and was responsible for creating a monthly newsletter to all employees. We worked hard to produce that newsletter, using a writer, a graphic designer, and a photographer to get it done every month. It featured news that we believed all employees needed to know and was a little *top heavy*, that is, it mostly featured the corporate positions on matters. It took lots of time and a significant budget. But, one day, I learned that it wasn't as popular as a photocopied rag that one division sent out routinely. They proudly called their rag, "Babies, bowling and bullshit." This publication included employee information such as the births of children, marriages, and personal achievements. We then added this information, as submitted by employees, to our publications. I'm certain many employees read that page of our publication first.

I learned a good lesson from that: communication is critical in corporations, employees have their own interests, and communication interests cannot be controlled. Be that as it may, although companies can't and shouldn't control the interests of their employees, they can and should make every effort to communicate vital information while also addressing the interests of employees. The CEO can have weekly breakfasts with employees; the executives can have similar meetings and can practice *Management By Walking Around*. The organization can provide daily bulletins and bi-weekly or monthly newsletters. Certainly, the firm can use more sophisticated means, such as broadcast e-mail and streaming video, as well as video conferencing.

To be effective, however, corporate communications must contain useful, relevant, and honest content, and these communications must be available to all. For this to happen, the executive leadership must have a predisposition to open, honest, and timely communication. Such communication won't guarantee a good workplace, but it will lead to that end.

Open communication allows management to understand the needs and concerns of employees by being aware of and acting on these concerns to build a better work environment, ultimately improving productivity. Likewise, as employees learn why changes are being made and what future plans are being considered, employees feel invested in the company. Beware companies that do not value open communication.

Ask the person who interviews you to answer this important question about communication. Or, if you have time and you're at the firm, look around for some of the communication tools. In all probability, you'll be given some of the company's printed materials in your interview packet. Regardless of how you come upon these materials, look them over carefully. They reveal things to you about the corporate culture, issues they consider important, they're top of the page and those that are meaningless, bottom corner, last page, or not mentioned at all.

Companion Questions to This One
    10. Does the company have rituals?

ASK ABOUT THE COMPANY   29

Question 12

Does the Company Value Diversity?

We live in a global society. This is indisputable. Some large American companies are doing more business outside America than inside. Over 3,500 multinationals are based in the United States. 40,000 U.S. firms do business with overseas companies, and most of the world's great banks lie outside the United States.

We live in a diverse society. In the 1970s, only 12 percent of the workforce in America was black, Hispanic, or Asian-American. By 1990, the workforce consisted of over 25 percent of those groups. Now, 37 percent of the workforce is composed of minorities. By the middle of this century, one half of the workforce will be comprised of those groups[5]. Will you work in Miami? If you do, you know that almost 70 percent of the workforce is Hispanic. The same holds true for Washington DC.

New technologies, not the least of which is the Internet, have opened the world to people from all cultures. The person or company that is not willing to learn about, respect, and embrace new cultures will not succeed. And, consequently, you would be ill-advised to accept an offer from an organization that cannot offer obvious evidence of its appreciation and nurturing of diverse groups.

Ask for specific information about programs, services, and opportunities related to diverse groups of people.

- How many managers from senior management are minorities?
- Do mentoring programs exist to support minority advancement into management positions?
- Does your company have programs within minority communities to help them enter college or internship programs for future employment in the company?

---

[5] https://whattobecome.com/blog/diversity-in-the-workplace-statistics/#:~:text =By%202020%2C%20minorities%20in%20the,US%20workforce%20by%20 next%20year.

Don't let the pictures on the website or the company newsletter fool you. Good PR with good casting does not equal a diverse workplace. You need to witness actual evidence of diversity within the company, particularly in senior management.

Companion Questions to This One

13. What is the organization's board make-up and involvement?

14. Does the company have programs to develop and promote minorities?

20. Is there a union at the organization?

Question 13

What Is the Organization's Board Makeup and Involvement?

You can expect different answers to this question, depending upon whether you interview with a for-profit or a not-for-profit. With the for-profit, you will be interested to know the kinds of talent and influence represented by the board of directors. General Dynamics had both Colin Powell, former U.S. Secretary of State, and Charlotte Beers, former Under Secretary of State, as board members. These two famous and influential people undoubtedly attended few meetings and voted on only a few issues, probably profit sharing. However, their presence on the board lent no small weight to the firm's prestige.

If you are considering working at a nonprofit, the questions of board makeup and involvement are as critical. Ask: What kind of talent and influence exists on the board, and what roles do these board members play?

All too often, board members, especially with nonprofits, believe they have operational authority. For instance, I once worked at a hospital in a small town where the board of trustees was comprised of the most powerful and wealthy people in the community. They caused more than one CEO to leave town because of their almost daily interference in the operations (and I don't necessarily mean surgical operations) at the hospital. But, this was a small town, and those board members owned the car dealerships, the real estate, and the McDonald's, Wendy's, and Burger King franchises. They were big fish in a small pond.

However, on the other side of things, you do not want a board that gives senior management free reign. At a health care organization in Pittsburgh, senior management made financial decisions, including the acquisition of hospitals and a medical school in another market that put the organization in a financial crisis. To cover losses, they then accessed restricted funds sending the entire organization into bankruptcy. The board impressed by the rapid growth of the organization failed to monitor the financial solvency of the organization. As bankruptcy ensued, the courts replaced the entire board because they did not perform their fiduciary duty. Had they overseen the financial status of the organization, bankruptcy and the ensuing loss of jobs would not have occurred. So, boards do play an important role in a company's operation.

You may, of course, find this information before you go on your interview. As with financial information, this information is a matter of record. Use the Internet, annual reports, the business media, among other sources, and find out who's on the board of the company for which you might someday work, find out how involved the board is in overseeing financial decisions and the strategic planning of the organization.

Companion Questions to This One

12. Does the company value diversity?

14. Does the company have programs to develop and promote minorities?

20. Is there a union at the organization?

Question 14

Does the Company Have Programs to Develop and Promote Minorities?

If you are guided by statistics alone, you will see that women and minorities make up a growing portion of the workforce, and that portion will likely continue to grow. This includes Hispanics, African Americans, Asians, lesbian, gay, bisexual, transgender and queer (LGBTQ), and others.

The U.S. workforce is, indeed, becoming more diverse, according to a report by the Center for American Progress. In a recent study, they found that people of color made up 36 percent of the labor force. Furthermore, 64 percent in the labor force were non-Hispanic white; 16 percent were Hispanic; 12 percent were African American; and 5 percent were Asian.

As of June 2020, women account for 47 percent of the labor force, that is over 72 million women over age 16, compared to over 82 million men over age 16, who account for 53 percent of the labor force.

People with disabilities make important contributions to our economy, but their talents are under-used. Eleven percent of Americans have a disability, but only 21 percent of those are in workforce. The unemployment rate of people with disabilities is 15 percent, compared to the rest of the workforce at 8.7 percent. Companies need to put effort into understanding the ways the workplace can be re-designed to allow handicapped workers to participate in the workforce. Often, these changes are easily made.

As for corporate boardrooms, forget it. At Fortune 500 companies, only 21 people of color are CEOs, 4 percent. Four are black (0.8 percent); nine are Asian (1.8 percent); and six are Latino (1.2 percent). And, more troubling, only four are female people of color, representing just 0.8 percent of all Fortune 500 CEOs. As the study said, women make up nearly half of the labor force today, but only 18 Fortune 500 CEOs (3.6 percent) are female.

Gay and transgender workers represent 6 percent of the workforce, and they have little representation in seats of power[6].

So, ask about opportunities for diverse peoples; it will make the organization stronger and your decision easier.

Companion Questions to This One
    12. Does the company value diversity?
    13. What is the organization's board makeup and involvement?
    20. Is there a union at the organization?

[6] https://www.americanprogress.org/issues/economy/reports/2012/07/12/11938/the-state-of-diversity-in-todays-workforce/

SECTION 2

Ask Appropriate Business Questions

Questions 15

How Is the Organization Positioned in the Market?

When you walk into a retail drug store, you will find many brands of shampoo. One is for dry hair, one is for oily hair, one is for color-treated hair, one is for thick hair, one is for thinning hair, one is for curly hair, one is for straight hair. One has argon oil, another has shea oil, one is for dandruff, one is for men. The same holds true for body wash. One is for dry skin, one for oily skin, one for breakout-prone skin, and on and on. This is positioning, products that want a uniqueness and appeal to targeted audiences. They want to be known differently by the laws of positioning (see "Positioning" by Trout and Ries).

Positioning informs you of a company's place in the market relative to its competitors and in the minds of its customers. It provides differentiation; customers choose a company's product because they identify with its positioning. You may be thinking, "Why is this important to me?" Customers buy a company's product because positioning tells them, this product meets my needs. Good positioning means more customers, means more revenue, means a financially stable company.

When you are being interviewed, ask the company representative how the company is positioned. How is Microsoft positioned? Microsoft is the largest and most trusted and successful maker of computer operating systems in the world. How is the Syracuse Housing Authority positioned?

How is the Cleveland Museum positioned? How is Oracle positioned? If you are going to accept a position in one of these organizations, ask the positioning question!

Companion Questions to This One

    16. How do you define the organization's market and share of market?

    17. Who are the company's main competitors?

Question 16

How Do You Define the Organization's Market and Share of Market?

Before you join, find out what market the company is in and what its share of that market is. Ask if the organization is in a new, growing, stable, declining, or dying market.

So, why should you, a programmer or policy analyst, want to know about the market and market share? Knowledge truly is power. You will want to join the company and move through the ranks. You need to ask important business questions. Market share, and other such questions, is important to know. In other words, you want to be a business person, for-profit or not-for profit.

Additionally, you should focus your employment search in companies in growing or stable markets. Clearly, it would be unwise to seek employment with a company that makes videocassette recorder (VCR) or cassette tapes, unless they have engineered them for a new usage. Particularly in the early and late stages of your career, you want to find employment with a growing, stable company offering a needed product or service. Perhaps after you have some experience you might risk working for a start-up or a company repositioning itself, but don't waste precious years of your career with a company unable to compete in the market. You can learn the answer to this question by looking at business publications such as *Forbes, Fortune, Business Week, Advertising Age*, and many others. Or, surf the Internet. You should have no trouble finding the answer.

Companion Questions to This One
   15. How is the organization positioned in the market?
   17. Who are the company's main competitors?

Question 17

Who Are the Company's Main Competitors?

Vito Corleone told his son, Michael, in the popular movie, *The Godfather*, "Keep your friends close but your enemies closer." Better business advice was never uttered!

You could call your competition *The Enemy!* They want what you have and make no secret of it. If you went out of business, they would not be sad. They develop new products and services to attract the same customers you're after. It makes sense, therefore, to know as much as possible about them.

Ask the person who interviews you about the company's competition. Anyone in the company should know this quickly and accurately. They should also pride themselves in knowing about their competition. As a former football and wrestling coach, I know that we all compete better when our competition is stronger. Even Bill Gates has to be comforted to know that Larry Ellison wants to eat his lunch. It keeps Bill moving faster!

Keeping track of the competition makes a company ever-mindful of the changing needs of its customers. To meet those needs before the competition makes the company innovative, agile, and growing, traits that encourage success.

Certainly, you can learn this information by researching the company on your own time. Read the business publications mentioned previously, *Forbes, Fortune, Business Week*, and so forth. And, as you read about the company's competition, evaluate how strong is the competition, is it more aggressive in the market, is it more innovative. At the end of your research, you may find you want to interview with the competition.

Companion Questions to This One

15. How is the organization positioned in the market?

16. How do you define the organization's market and share of market?

SECTION 3

Ask What Really Goes On Inside the Company

Question 18

Has the Organization Ever Faced a Crisis? What Was the Crisis and How Did the Company Respond?

Any employee of Johnson & Johnson (J&J) would be happy to be asked this question. The J&J response to the Tylenol crisis of the 1980s is considered the model for crisis management. In brief, someone (who has never been identified) poisoned Tylenol with cyanide, resulting in the deaths of seven people and a nationwide recall of Tylenol. Because of its mission and values, J&J recalled millions of dollars' worth of the product and suffered millions of dollars of loss. However, J&J leaders were concerned, first, about the public (see mission and values). They addressed the matter of the poisonings quickly and openly. They cooperated with the authorities from day one. And, they have benefited ever since.

Crises can say a lot about any organization and its leadership. How do the top people act under pressure? Ask New Yorkers about Rudy Giuliani during the 9/11 attacks on the World Trade Center in 2001. He is considered one of the heroes for his fast and decisive actions. Then there's Exxon and the Valdez oil spill, which damaged 200 miles of coastline. In the aftermath of this spill, investigators found that Exxon's ship did not have the navigational equipment to avoid the wreck and failed to respond to the spill in the important first hours. You do not want to be working for a company that the public continues to associate with environmental disaster.

To react well to a crisis, a company must have a crisis plan that they regularly review and update. Successful companies prepare for a crisis long before it occurs, so even if a company has never responded to a crisis, the company representative should acknowledge that a crisis plan exists.

Get the picture? Exxon blew it on that occasion.

Companion Questions to This One

19. How do problems get resolved in the organization?

Question 19

How Do Problems Get Resolved in the Organization?

Not every organization faces poisonings and terror attacks, but all organizations have more problems than they know what to do with, even the very best companies. Yes, even Ben and Jerry have to wrestle once in a while to straighten things out.

So, ask the interviewer about company processes for problem resolution. Ask him or her to identify a particular problem and its resolution. Don't worry about being out of place. Ask these questions. You are about to make a very important decision in your life. You will spend most of your waking hours either at, or thinking about, this place. You have the right to know how you and the company will confront the issues that invariably the best-run companies encounter. As always, however, speak with dignity and respect and not like an arrogant troublemaker.

As organizations grow and modernize, they must find new ways to operate. Employees often must often take on new responsibilities. Management must deal with the inevitable problem that new ways of doing this present. Organizations that encourage input from employees weather these transitions much better than those that expect employees to suffer silently.

Is there a suggestion box? Does HR make available an online chat? Does a formal grievance procedure exist? How are problems resolved?

Companion Questions to This One

18. Has the organization ever faced a crisis? What was the crisis, and how did the company deal with this crisis?

Question 20

Is There a Union at the Organization?

The existence of a union in an organization changes some of the dynamics of employee interactions; they can be more complex. If a union exists, you have the right to know if you will be required to join. If not, will you interact with the union? If so, how?

In my first job, I taught English in a junior high school. At the end of my first year of teaching, the teachers formed an *association*, which looked a lot like a union (and eventually became one). I needed two years of successful teaching to gain tenure and told my dad that I would likely cross any picket line. Union man that he was (having been elected president of the local boilermakers union), he flew into a tirade, telling me that I was stupid, and that I would forever be labeled *scab*. As it turned out, I never had to make the choice because the teachers didn't walk.

Most of my career I spent as *management* and was required to walk across picket lines. My father would have rolled over in his grave had he known. During his lifetime, unions played an important role in ensuring safe working conditions and fair pay. I understood that I was doing exactly as I was expected to do. I was comfortable with it.

Often, management must cross picket lines so that a company can continue to exist during the strike and can ramp up production quickly when the strike has ended.

You will need to understand your relationship with a union, should one exist at your place of work.

Question 21

What Do the Workspaces Look Like in the Company?

I have my own office, always have. I have never worked in an open, shared workspace. That's exactly the way I like it. I ask my students to schedule appointments if they wish to speak with me, no walking in the door. Likewise, I respect people's spaces even if their workspace is a cubicle.

By all means, ask your interviewer what your workspace will be, if you are to be hired. You need to decide how you feel about that. Being in a cubicle in the middle of a large space with no access to windows or natural light may be a death sentence to some people. Ask, too, if you receive an answer you don't like, if that space is negotiable.

American companies have largely abandoned offices in favor of open workspaces. Although this allows for more open communication and transparency, it presents problems. Many employees complain of interruptions and problems concentrating. Aware of this, some employers have additional quiet spaces to retreat to. Most evidence points to a remote workforce, one that is typically working from home in information jobs.

Where you reside for a minimum of eight hours a day is a very serious matter, just ask people who have worked in cramped, dingy settings. Ask anyone who has ever worked in a *sick building*, for that matter. Ask not the CEO, who enjoys space and privacy, but the OCE, office cubicle employee! Cubicle equals no privacy; I don't care how much it levels the organization and creates integration. Forget it. Give me an office.

Companion Questions to This One
    22. How would you describe the company environment?
    23. Is there a corporate dress code?

Question 22

How Would You Describe the Company Environment?

My father worked for the railroad all his life. He was a boilermaker/welder for the Pennsylvania Railroad, which became the Penn Central, which became Conrail. He worked in both the Juniata Shops in Altoona, PA (home of the world-famous *Horseshoe Curve*) and in the Samuel Rea Shops in Hollidaysburg, PA.

My father didn't say much, but one thing he said to me was, "You'll never work for the railroad." To say he didn't like his work would be an understatement; he complained that the railroad shops where he welded eight hours a day were "too hot in the summer and too cold in the winter." A union man, he also complained mightily about management, whose environments, he felt, were insulated from the extremes of weather he experienced through every season.

He also complained about the noise and dirt. He should have complained louder, for as it turned out he succumbed to cancer probably exacerbated by exposure to the asbestos he worked with.

Before you take employment, learn as much as you can about the physical environment of the buildings in which you will spend your days (or nights, or both). Will you not accept a job if you don't like the workspace? Possibly. But, find out, anyway! Visit the company, if you can. Ask the people who work there about the work environment. Are they permitted to post photographs of relatives or relics of their hobbies. Are all workspaces uniform indicating an autocratic environment?

Companion Questions to This One
    21. What do the workspaces look like in the company?
    23. Is there a corporate dress code?

Question 23

Is There a Corporate Dress Code?

All companies have a dress code, some are more formal and are written in the employee manual. Others are less formal and may only include certain things that may not be worn. Dress codes over time have become less formal. However, more conservative organizations tend to have more formal requirements for the attire of their employees, mostly suits. Whatever the accepted dress code, whether formal or casual, you must feel comfortable dressing in that manner.

Dress codes may change for specific situations that occur in an organization. I once worked at a for-profit that had issued a public stock offering over NASDAQ. The CEO knew that the stock would move if brokers understood the company and the value of its stock. So, the CEO put into place an aggressive plan to familiarize a select group of brokers with our company, a television production firm.

Our product was a creative service, and therefore somewhat suspect in the eyes of the financial people of Pittsburgh, who thought more in terms of slabs of steel, so we hosted a group of area stock brokers at the city's old and revered Duquesne Club to introduce them to our *product.*

In this august setting, we drank cocktails, shook hands, made small talk, and showed a fast-paced, creative capabilities video. After the brokers had left with copies of the video and company t-shirts and ball caps, we huddled to debrief. The CEO was satisfied but scolded the chief financial officer for wearing a sports coat with no tie, and not a suit, to the event. Many brokers have no fashion sense; however, they recognize the uniform of the conservative financial community, a suit. Both the CEO and CFO knew that, and the CEO wanted to make an impression. He said, "You can always remove your tie if you want to loosen up but you can't make one magically appear if you haven't worn one."

Within a company, different expectations may exist for different areas of a company in terms of attire. As I said earlier, at the television production company, the creative types were expected to dress in the latest funky attire. The people on the business side were expected to dress in business attire. The rules were not written down anywhere but were as inviolable as any of the strictest regulations. Knowing the expected daily attire for your job area will help you to fit in should you be offered and accept a position in a company.

Companion Questions to This One
    21. What do the workspaces look like in the company?
    22. How would you describe the company environment?

Question 24

Who Are the Corporate Heroes/Heroines?

What Are the Corporate Myths?

Every organization has memorable people. Usually, it's the founders. Often, it's the rebels. These are people who have left their mark on the organization and are spoken about reverentially, often in whispers, mostly after they have gone, of their own choosing or through martyrdom. Many have passed into myth.

I knew a teacher once, let's call him Mr. Young, who, in the late 1960s, inspired his students with his energy, youth, daring, and disdain for authority. He wore his hair long and dressed casually. He openly represented every impulse young people were encouraged to repress. His young students related to him enthusiastically, particularly when the authorities of the school sought to bridle him, unwittingly feeding his popularity. His colleagues admired him but watched and quietly awaited his demise. He finally left, of his own accord, and in his leaving became the stuff of faculty room conversations and student memories. The rebel with a cause!

Mr. Young carried the standard for a new thinking, a new way of acting. In his small way, in his small town with his important, but minor position, he showed a small group of people a new way of thinking and acting. He became their hero.

Every organization, regardless of size, has such characters. Ask about them. Most likely you'll hear about the heroes. However, in innovative companies, you will likely hear about the rebel who dared to try a different approach to a problem. If that new approach resulted in success, you'll hear about that rebel. When you hear about the hero or the rebel, you learn about the types of behaviors encouraged and rewarded in that company.

Ask How the Place Is Managed

Question 25

What Characteristics Does the Model Employee of the Company Possess?

If the person who interviews you has responsibility for recruitment, he or she has undoubtedly seen many people come and go and could, therefore, summarize the profile of the typical hire. If the person who interviews you makes the hiring decision, he or she should certainly be able to provide that profile.

You need to listen carefully to the description. Is this someone who will be asked to conform rigidly, take no risks, and work collaboratively? Is this someone who is expected to be mature, self-motivated, self-directed, and responsive? What exactly are the characteristics that make a person successful in this company?

Perhaps it's someone like Mr. Young, described in the previous chapter. He was an iconoclast. He represented a new kind of thinking. He was innovative, and that made him frightening to some people. Or, the ideal person may be the one who keeps his head down and his nose out of trouble. Or, the person may be someone willing to devote a lot of unpaid overtime to the company. Or, the person may be a leader who brings people together collaboratively. Ask and consider, do I have the characteristics they value in an employee?

Jim, a friend of mine, took a job with an actuarial firm. After a few weeks, the CEO called Jim into the office and noted that he left at five each day. Jim agreed that happened. The CEO informed Jim that his employees saw themselves as warriors, working 10- and 12-hour days. Jim informed the CEO he completed his work by five each day and did not see himself as a warrior and quit. He has worked quite successfully in his replacement job for over 20 years.

Be sure a company's model employee fits with your vision of a model employee.

Companion Questions to This One

26. What skills are valued most?

27. How would you describe the successful manager in the company?

Question 26

What Skills Are Valued Most?

If you're applying for a programmer's position, then obviously programming skills will be highly valued. If you're applying for a policy analyst's position, you must have some skill in analytical thinking. And, you understand that your skill level must match with the position you hope to be hired for in the organization.

I worked in a health care system where strategic thinking and planning were the most valued skills, although no one stated this. Financial management ranked equally with the strategic thinking and planning. However, finances were left pretty much to the bean counters. Too much understanding of finance actually pigeonholed a person as a finance expert only. Critical thinking, however, was prized, as was the ability to construct a tight planning document.

Fortunately for me, writing and speaking were also valued. I succeeded because of these strengths and my quick understanding that I had to bolster my strategic thinking and planning skills. I mastered the questions: What is our objective? How will we measure our success at achieving that objective? What will this cost? How will we measure our return on investment? Add to those questions another few and they will serve you well: Who are the target audiences? How do we describe them? What are their needs? What is our timeframe for this project?

In summary, you may think you know the skills required for the position that interests you, but you're better off if you can have them articulated. Ask your potential manager what skills are most valued in the organization and particularly for the position in question.

Companion Questions to This One
   25. What characteristics does the model employee of the company possess?
   27. How would you describe the successful manager in the company?

Question 27

How Would You Describe the Successful Manager in the Company?

You will want to know as much as possible about the management styles of the people for whom you are likely to work. Forget theory X-Y-Z. Get an honest and practical profile. "Our managers expect results but are willing to listen and to help. They mentor. They care. They provide resources for individual growth."

Perhaps the best manager is the one who communicates well, who collaborates, who does not micromanage. They have cultural competence; they give credit where it's due. They make objective decisions; they help people grow and learn.

According to an article on the LinkedIn website, "A Gallup poll of more than 1 million employed U.S. workers concluded that the No. 1 reason people quit their jobs is a bad boss or immediate supervisor." About 75 percent of workers who voluntarily left their jobs did so because of their bosses and not the position itself. In spite of how good a job may be, people will quit if the reporting relationship is not healthy. "People leave managers not companies. . .in the end, turnover is mostly a manager issue.[1]"

The best managers have a good intelligence quotient (IQ) and a better emotional quotient (EQ), emotional intelligence. They know how to interpret and manage their emotions, and they can recognize the emotions of others. They treat employees with dignity and respect even in difficult circumstances. They encourage staff development through positive interactions. They refrain from making derogatory remarks even in jest. These kinds of managers exist. Find yourself one!

Listen closely as the person interviewing you describes valued management skills. Make sure you fit with the description of your potential manager.

Companion Questions to This One

    25. What characteristics does the model employee of the company possess?

    26. What skills are valued most?

---

[1] https://linkedin.com/pulse/employees-dont-leave-companies-managers-brigette-hyacinth/

Question 28

Does the Organization Have a Recognition-Rich Environment?

We all like to be told we're doing something well. Actually, we like the public acknowledgment more than we like the financial rewards (although they're not hard to take, either). Who has been named "Employee of the Month" and not enjoyed seeing his or her picture hanging in the lobby? Who has been cited for outstanding work and not enjoyed a privileged parking place for a month at the front of the building? Who has completed a tough project on time and not enjoyed lunch with the CEO?

I have often said that money is a negative motivator. That is, when people come forward and say that they want to quit their jobs because they don't make enough, they are usually disguising some other complaint (not enough challenge, not enough growth opportunity, not enough recognition).

If people love their jobs and receive recognition for their good work, they will work for free. When I worked for a television production company, we produced television commercials, rock concerts, NFL football, NHL hockey. We had celebrities in and out of our studios. We enjoyed a relaxed and creative atmosphere. People wanted to work at our company. And, they were willing to work for little or nothing! Certainly you want to be rewarded financially for your contribution to an organization's bottom line, but recognition is equally important.

One young man, an English major from the University of Pittsburgh, who had graduated and was bartending at a nearby tavern where he met many of the company staff, worked at our video production firm for free on his off time so as to be involved with the work we were doing. Eventually, we hired him, and he went on to produce Pittsburgh Pirate baseball for broadcast where his name was regularly featured on the broadcast credits.

Research funded by Make Their Day, an employee motivation firm, and Badgeville, a gamification company, surveyed 1,200 U.S. employees from a broad cross-section of industries. Among the study's highlights:

83 percent of respondents said recognition for contributions was more fulfilling than any rewards or gifts.

88 percent found praise from managers very or extremely motivating[2]. Money is a negative motivator. Recognition has real value!

Companion Questions to This One

29. What is the organization's retention rate?
30. What opportunities exist for training and staff development?
31. Does the organization have profit sharing, gain sharing, an ESOP?

[2] https://psychologytoday.com/us/blog/mind-the-manager/201306/newemployee-study-shows-recognition-matters-more-money

Question 29

What Is the Organization's Retention Rate?

Remember: The Pareto principle is the *80–20* rule. In total, 80 percent of the company services or products are purchased by 20 percent of its customers. And, 80 percent of all the work is done by 20 percent of the staff, that sort of thing.

Compensation Force measured the level of total separations in the United States 2016 at 15.1 percent. In other words, 15.1 percent of the total U.S. workforce left their job in 2016. The separation rate includes employees who voluntarily quit a position, layoffs, retirements, and discharges.

SHRM predicted the annual turnover rate to be close to 19 percent and also assumed that the average cost-per-hire to fill a position at $4,129. Some studies show that replacing an entry-level position can cost up to 40 percent of an employee's salary.

Losing good employees is expensive, and in some cases avoidable[3].

Satisfied employees stay. Sure, life circumstances change, people begin families, retire, or move to warmer climates or to greener financial pastures. That is to be expected and is reflected in data on retention. But, sometimes, a low turnover rate doesn't automatically suggest a great place to work. My dad worked for the railroad for 35 years and I venture to say that he hated all 35. I guess he thought he couldn't do anything else.

But, satisfied, challenged, and engaged employees do not leave the company. They hardly ever think about it, in fact. They are too busy being challenged and enjoying their work.

Ask about the turnover (or retention). The good companies volunteer this information!

Companion Questions to This One

28. Does the organization have a *recognition-rich* environment?

30. What opportunities exist for training and staff development?

31. Does the organization have profit sharing, gain sharing, an ESOP?

---

[3] https://dailypay.com/blog/employee-retention-rate/#:~:text=As%20mentioned %20earlier%2C%2010,%2C%20high%2Dperforming%20team%20members

Question 30

What Opportunities Exist for Training and Staff Development?

Only organizations lacking good common sense fail to budget, and budget well, for training and staff development.

Job skills change continuously. People want to progress. Change is natural. If this didn't happen, the *Shoe Factory Mentality* would set in.

What is the *Shoe Factory Mentality*? It can be described as mindless repetition and boredom. I saw it firsthand when I worked a summer in a shoe factory. I watched people sit at machines and perform the same tasks over and over, punching out the soles of shoes, running sewing machines around leather, rewarded by piece work sewn at greater speeds. They were an unhappy lot. They faced the prospect of doing the same routine over and over and over until they retired.

The smart organizations invest heavily in training and education for their employees. Most have educational reimbursements. If they don't, they should. Make sure you check this out with a prospective employer, especially if your job faces automation.

Niall McKinney, president of AVADO, a learning company based in London, noted that as jobs automate, employers may need to help employees reskill to match the new jobs that will appear. "We think people are spending more because the skills required in roles are changing very quickly," he said.

As more jobs become automated, employers need to help employees re-deploy in new or more advanced areas. Around 32 percent of current workers aged 16 to 54, regardless of their position, may need to retrain within the next 12 years, according to McKinsey reports cited by AVADO.

Kelly Palmer, CLO at Degreed, a talent development company, said in an e-mail that cost is not an excuse for not training employees. "The reality is that today anybody can learn any topic, from any device, anywhere in the world at low to no cost," she said. With so much content available, she added, "it's more about encouraging and allowing employees to spend time learning[4]."

---

[4] https://hrdive.com/news/why-employers-are-spending-more-on-learningand-development/545903/

Additionally, education often opens doors to advancement. Without it, opportunities are limited. So, your future in one way or another often depends on the education opportunities your company provides for you on site or through reimbursement for classes. Successful companies retrain valued employees. Ask if the company you are interviewing with offers these opportunities.

Companion Questions to This One

28. Does the organization have a *recognition-rich* environment?

29. What is the organization's retention rate?

31. Does the organization have profit sharing, gain sharing, an ESOP?.

Question 31

Does the Organization Have Profit Sharing, Gain Sharing, an ESOP?

I worked in a not-for-profit where we had *Gain Sharing*. We couldn't, of course, call it *Profit Sharing*, so what was made on the bottom line and shared the organization called by another name.

I enjoyed this benefit. I remember getting a pretty nice check at the end of the year. Some executives got really nice checks. I'm talking about checks worth several thousand dollars. As I recall, the CEO was a little embarrassed about the million or so dollars this not-for-profit shared with its management and hoped it would not be made public through the media, that never happened.

Most for-profits have profit sharing, and rightly so. Or, they have generous ESOPs, employee stock option plans. Those are beneficial as long as the stock has value. Ask the people who may have worked at ENRON and had its stock. It was bad enough that its 401K invested in ENRON. You may want to ask your employer, as well, where it invests its employees' 401K funds.

Research indicates that shared capitalism (profit shares, group bonuses) can also improve job satisfaction. This is the case even when controlling for the additional income a worker can derive from group incentive plans. This suggests that workers derive value from sharing ownership in their firm over and above the value they get from making additional money. The effect is partly related to the warm glow employees feel in response to the *gift* of free or discounted shares, and partly to the effect ESOPs have in dampening the *bad* aspects of a job. Importantly, individual performance-related pay plans do not have this positive well-being effect—they can incentivize through income, but they don't affect worker well-being in the same way as shared capitalism programs[5]. Those programs make employees feel that they benefit from the extra effort they put into their jobs.

---

[5] https://hbr.org/2016/12/profit-sharing-boosts-employee-productivity-and-satisfaction

Companion Questions to This One

    28. Does the organization have a *recognition-rich* environment?

    29. What is the organization's retention rate?

    30. What opportunities exist for training and staff development?

Question 32

How Are Customer Relations Handled?

Why would you ask a question like this? Isn't this the responsibility of the marketing department? What does customer relations have to do with employee relations?

For one thing, a company should treat everyone the same way. If they treat their customers well, they are likely to treat their employees well. If they have systems for treating their customers well, they are likely to have systems for treating their employees well.

However, unfortunately, this is not often the case. Some companies erroneously view employees as disposable. And, they soon view customers as needing their services. This mentality soon leads to a company's demise. Well-run companies value employees and customers equally. They follow philosophies that make people feel their needs are important to the company, and the company strives to meet them. Everyone in the organization has an important role in marketing.

"For a consumer faced with a glut of choice and their own rising expectations, the experience a company provides is increasingly the differentiator between brands. In fact, the recently launched second edition of Salesforce's 'State of the Connected Customer' which reveals that 80% of customers say the experience a company provides is as important as its products and services and 76% say it is easier than ever to take their business else-where."

"Salesforce's research also finds 76% of customers expect companies to understand their needs and expectations and 84% of customers say being treated like a person, not a number, is very important to winning their business[6]."

Everyone has choices just like companies. Each company can choose to be pleasant and respectful and helpful, or they can choose to be complacent, uncaring, and unresponsive to customer needs and concerns. Find how this company treats people it; foretells how they treat employees.
Companion Questions to This One

33. Does the organization support any cause?

---

[6] https://marketingweek.com/how-customer-experience-impacts-the-bottomline/

Question 33

Does the Organization Support Any Cause?

These days the enlightened for-profit organizations are partnering with not-for-profits to be socially accountable. Since the Statue of Liberty Fund and American Express partnered to raise money for restoration of the statue, many corporations have collaborated to do the right thing.

Ben & Jerry's represents a good case-in-point. Ben & Jerry's and its employees contribute to many social causes, including the environment, nuclear waste clean-up, mental health support, children's issues, and wild lands preservation, among many others.

Usually, companies with a conscience, companies that are interested in more than themselves and their profit, also have more interest in their employees. Try to choose a company to work for that works for others.

"…consumers aren't the only group that can benefit from and appreciate a well-executed cause marketing campaign." Consider these statistics:

About 53 percent of workers and 72 percent of students say a job where they can make an impact is very important or essential to their happiness, with the students ranking it third in overall importance and only 1 percent behind marriage (according to the *Net Impact: What Workers Want* study by Rutgers University).

Increasing the engagement level in a 10,000-person organization by 5 percent can boost profits by an estimated $40+ million (according to Taleo Research)[7].

Feeling good about the social impact of your organization makes you feel better about contributing your talents to that organization, in other words job satisfaction.

Companion Questions to This One
32. How are customer relations handled?

_____
[7] https://frontstream.com/blog/using-cause-marketing-to-improve-employee-engagement

Question 34

How Flexible Is the Company?

Let's hope the era of sweatshops has ended, all over the world. Let's hope employers exist that allow employees to job share, telecommute, and re-design their jobs. Let's hope you can find an organization that allows flexible scheduling, compressed work weeks, and any other adjustments that are appropriate and necessary for you to perform your work well.

"Lean start-ups are moving with purpose, speed and agility to reshape markets. By contrast, most major corporations are heavily layered, bureaucratic, and stifled by complex webs of reporting lines that weigh-down leadership and smother talent.

To compete in this environment, we believe organizational structure must evolve to unlock the potential within enterprises and unleash the latent power in networked teams. Under this new model, predictable efficiency gives way to rapid adaptability. Smaller is actually better. Focused teams with resources, air-cover, and real decision authority will always be 'faster to market' than heavily structured groups that require approvals before each step[8]."

The recent pandemic transformed flexibility from a desirable perk into a powerful people practice, one that is expected to endure well after COVID-19 is in the rearview mirror, according to recent research from Mercer.

In another article, Lauren Mason, principal at Mercer, explains that the pandemic has reshaped both employer and employee expectations regarding flexibility. While flexibility *from work* primarily was offered through a combination of emergency leave and paid sick time and flexibility *at work* featured options such as work from home and job sharing, flexibility overall today has taken on a new meaning, as a result of nationwide school and office closures.

"As employers look towards reinvention, pre-COVID approaches to flexibility may no longer be sufficient," Mason says.

---

[8] https://www2.deloitte.com/global/en/pages/human-capital/articles/gx-unlocking-the-flexible-organization.html

Mercer reports, in fact, that over 83 percent of organizations will continue workplace flexibility at a greater scale postpandemic. She adds that COVID-19 has resulted in a great *experiment* for many organizations around flexibility, noting that office and school closures have resulted in real-time innovation… "over 90 percent of employers say productivity has stayed the same or increased as a result of remote working[9]."

Flexibility can increase your job satisfaction immeasurably. Working in other ways, whether from home or other places, offers employees flexibility and often increases their output. You need to know how flexible your company is.

Companion Questions to This One

    35. Is the organization parent-friendly?

---

[9] https://hrexecutive.com/how-covid-19-will-redefine-workplace-flexibility-forever/

Question 35

Is the Organization Parent-Friendly?

These days employers must provide family leave. But, that doesn't make them parent-friendly.

Ask your potential employer if it has a day care facility on site or the benefit package that allows for funds to be set aside for child care. Ask if it has facilities for breast pumping. Ask if employees may leave in mid-day if they receive a call that a child has become ill. Ask for specific examples of employees, even executives, who have families and who may have had family issues that required leave or an altered work schedule.

Depending on your age and marital status, this question may or may not be critical to you. Nonetheless, the answers to the question can be equally revealing for unmarried or unattached persons.

According to a report by the Bureau of Labor Statistics, of the nearly 90 percent of American families with children in 2015, at least one parent was employed. For the working parents in these families, trying to find a balance between work obligations and family demands can be all-consuming and exhausting.

As a result, more and more workers now look for employers who understand that an individual's personal and professional life cannot always be distinctly compartmentalized. In fact, according to a 2014 report by The Council of Economic Advisers (a White House agency), a third of employees—including nearly 50 percent of working parents—have turned down a job because it conflicted with their family responsibilities.

As more owners in businesses of all sizes have become aware of this development, they have begun to implement a host of family-friendly policies that will help them recruit and retain the best possible employees, according to Sodexo's *2015* Workplace Trends Report. Some companies are beginning to offer benefits related to elder care also. These family-friendly policies are helping to increase employee morale, job satisfaction, and productivity while reducing absenteeism and disengagement[10].
Companion Questions to This One

34. How flexible is the company?

---

[10] https://businessnewsdaily.com/9614-family-friendly-workplace.html

Question 36

Does the Company Provide a New Employee Orientation?

Does the company provide a new employee orientation and, if so, how is it structured?

I have worked in organizations where the orientation lasted all day, often an awful, boring tedium. These orientations provided little important information about the employer. First, we saw the company video. Then, we sat through a series of unenthused speakers from various departments providing basic information in a perfunctory manner. If you weren't asleep after a human resources representative showed you an overhead projected rendition of your pay stub, you were surely asleep as the company nurse explained the various services available. Near lunchtime, most were awakened by the security department's demonstration of the fire extinguishers. When we sent someone off to the corporate employee orientation, we always sent them with pagers and promised to page them after the pay stub presentation.

My experiences notwithstanding, employee orientations can be very important if they are created so as to share the history, traditions, and culture of the company, if the executives participate and welcome the new hires, if useful information is provided and processes explained. Ask your interviewer about the information provided in orientation.

Research shows that orientations offer these benefits:
- Increase of retention of a pool of new, skilled, and capable employees, turning them into worthwhile long-term assets or investments of the organization. According to research, employee retention improves by 25 percent, thanks to effective new employee orientation programs.
- Improve the organization's ability to acclimate its new employees to the organization.
- Increase in the company's overall productivity and performance.
- Establishment of clear standards that help reduce risks of disputes and disagreements[11].

---

[11]   https://cleverism.com/10-tips-effective-new-employee-orientation/

Orientations can be an important vehicle to introduce a new hire to the company and make them familiar with its culture, mission, procedures, and benefits. They can ease the transition and help a new hire to become an important part of the organization.

Companion Questions to This One

37. Does the organization require employees to write goals?

38. How are employees evaluated?

39. Does a job description exist for this position?

SECTION 5

Ask How You Will Be Evaluated After You Join the Company

Question 37

Does the Organization Require Employees to Write Goals?

I worked in a system where the executives wrote a strategic plan that included goals to be achieved by each executive. The executives, in turn, shared that plan, and their goals, with their managers who were required to write goals that would support the larger effort while being related to every-day job duties. These managers shared their goals with their subordinates who, in turn, wrote goals designed to accomplish their specific duties while relating to management's goals. This created a beautiful system feeding the growth and success of the company.

The goal writing system required specific, measurable language and it was negotiable, in large part. That meant employees created a performance plan with their managers that allowed them to see their relationship to the whole. And, again, the goals were specific and measurable. The process also called for regular review of the goals and periodic adjustment. In a sense, it delivered self-fulfilling success.

You should look for an employer that measures performance through such a system. In any event, you need to know how your performance will be measured.

What do the experts say? "It's common knowledge that helping employees set and reach goals is a critical part of every manager's job," says Amy Gallo in the *Harvard Business Review*. "Employees want to see how their work contributes to larger corporate objectives, and setting the right targets makes this connection explicit for them, and for you, as their manager. Goal-setting is particularly important as a mechanism for providing ongoing and year-end feedback."

"Linda Hill, the Wallace Brett Donham Professor of Business Administration at the Harvard Business School and co-author of *Being the Boss: The 3 Imperatives for Becoming a Great Leader*, says 'A manager's job is to provide 'supportive autonomy' that's appropriate to the person's level of capability.' The key is to be hands-on while giving your people the room they need to succeed on their own."

Companion Questions to This One
   36. Does the company provide a new employee orientation?
   38. How are employees evaluated?
   39. Does a job description exist for this position?

Question 38

How Are Employees Evaluated?

The last thing you want is to have your performance, and hence your financial success, measured by arbitrary factors, such as your popularity. You want your measurement system to be as objective as possible. You want none of this—"Susie did a great job this year; everyone likes her." You're asking for trouble if you accept such a subjective and flawed evaluation system.

Of course, any measurement system has flaws and biases, just ask the people at GE who suffered with *Rank and Yank*. No system is completely objective and able to weed out the truly poor performers. Nonetheless, many companies strive to reduce biases by creating quantitative performance measurement.

I said earlier that I worked at a not-for-profit, religious-based health care system. This system flouted its mission to the public and to employees and asked that each employee goal-writer provide specific, measurable goals that included a *mission goal*. You might ask: How can mission be measured? Let me give you an example from my performance plan as an employee of that organization.

Mercy's mission was, in general, "to create a healthy community." Again, mission statements are global. For an organization to "create a healthy community," it would have to eliminate not only physical illness but societal illnesses as well. That means it would have to attack the problems of drug and alcohol abuse, child abuse, poverty, joblessness, and a host of other problems, such as illiteracy. Also, you'll remember that a Mercy values included "community" and "collaboration," among four others.

Having studied music, I volunteered at a not-for-profit called Youth Opportunities Unlimited (YOU). I volunteered to teach guitar. My mission goal, therefore, was written, "I will teach three students guitar within the year." I am happy to say that I wrote that goal for several years and, in fact, worked with many great not-for-profits in Pittsburgh to help young people change their lives through music.

Before you accept a job, be certain that you understand the evaluation system. Make certain it is based on objective criteria, and that you have some part in the performance plan's development and writing. After all, you will be measured against this plan.

Companion Questions to This One
    36. Does the company provide a new employee orientation?
    37. Does the organization require employees to write goals?
    39. Does a job description exist for this position?

Question 39

Does a Job Description Exist for This Position?

Almost every organization uses job descriptions. And, almost every job description contains the line "And other similar related duties." It is that line that allows the organization to have you perform the duties not specifically listed in the job description. Be that as it may, the job description tells an employee most of what the company expects. It may not be a perfect and complete description, but it explains things reasonably well.

I tell my students and friends not to accept a job that has no job description (and not to accept a job without a commitment from management to develop a written and negotiated performance plan, that is, set of goals). I recommend that any person being considered for a job ask to see the job description at an early interview, either the first or second. I suggest that any person who wants to accept a position with a company that does not have a written job description volunteer to write one, with input from the manager, immediately after accepting the job.

Hey, you are going to be evaluated. Your success in the company, and your earning power therein, will depend, to a large extent, on evaluations derived from your job description. Shouldn't they be based, as much as possible, on some objective criteria? Shouldn't a job description be used in your evaluations? Otherwise, how will you know if you've performed all of the duties expected of your position? How can you or your manager evaluate your performance without a description of the duties expected of your position?

Companion Questions to This One
  36. Does the company provide a new employee orientation?
  37. Does the organization require employees to write goals?
  38. How are employees evaluated?

Question 40

What Is the Typical Day and Workload Like for This Position?

You need as much information as the interviewer is able to give you so that you have a realistic idea of the work you will be expected to accomplish. If it's a new position, the information may be vague, but if it's an ongoing position, you should be given a concrete answer. You might also be told the status of the person who had the job.

What you'd like to hear, of course, is, "She was promoted to vice president (or some other lofty title)." You'd like to know that the organization mentors, coaches, and advances its people. It can be this way! Organizations can, in fact, coach their employees to greatness. Many don't, but that's another story.

You may hear, "She took a job with the competition." Or, you may hear that your predecessor took another job as a result of relocation or promotion, or left for personal reasons related to family. These are legitimate reasons. Few people any more work their whole lives for one company. And, just about everyone is flattered to have another company seek his/her services.

All too often, however, people leave because they can't handle the demands of the job. When this happens, the fault lies almost exclusively with the employer because of bad management, bad planning, or bad employee selection. Selecting a new employee is one of the most important decisions a company can make. Unfortunately, many make the decision too lightly, or they base the decision on the wrong qualities. And, potential employees make the decision equally lightly, especially the young and inexperienced. The best fit occurs when candidates and companies present themselves as openly and honest as possible.

Companion Questions to This One

    41. Have there been any lay-offs recently?

Question 41

Have There Been Any Lay-Offs Recently?

This speaks for itself. You need to know what job displacements have occurred, how many staff were effected, what caused the displacements, what was, or is, being done to avoid further displacements.

Also, listen to the language and tone the interviewer uses to answer. Remember that this person represents the company. His or her language and tone will reveal sensitivity or insensitivity to the victims of the displacement and the attitude of the executives. How this person reacts to any of your questions will likely reveal the actions, attitudes and opinions of the administration.

If there was a lay-off, how was it handled? I've been through four, three of which I helped to implement, and one of which I suffered through. I know the subject from both sides. I know that a lay-off isn't the worst thing in the world, but how it is executed can be. Even in organizations that espouse human dignity, lay-offs can go very badly.

Very bad lay-off processes make people feel valueless at a time when their self-esteem is low, anyway. Only the most caring organization can make a lay-off a less-than-catastrophic occurrence. In the best of circumstances with larger lay-offs, the organization offers displacement services, including counseling to help employees find new employment and deal with psychological issues related to lay-offs. This is an organization that cares about their employees, a place you would want to work.

In the late 1980s, Mellon Bank in Pittsburgh laid off over 500 people in a single day and several others in subsequent weeks. It was the first and largest lay-off in its history and resulted from bad foreign debt. Some of the employees had begun working for Mellon just out of college and at the time of the lay-off were in their 60s, just short of retirement. The bank set up counseling services to help people reboot their resumes, practice interviewing, and receive counseling. Although it wasn't their best memory, many employees were able to find employment though those efforts, significantly softening the blow.

Also, the organization's answer to "do you anticipate additional lay-offs" is very important. You do not want to give up a job or get oriented to a job only to be laid off a few months on the job.

Companion Questions to This One

40. What is the typical day and workload like for this position?

Question 42

What Techniques Does the Company Use to Increase Morale?

The answer to this question suggests not only how valued the employees are but how creative the management staff is.

Here's how my morale was increased. I teach at Carnegie Mellon University. It provides full tuition for any of my children who choose to go there (and are admitted). For any two children who choose to attend another school, Carnegie Mellon pays a percentage of that cost. Is that a great benefit, or what?! Talk about a morale booster!

Forms of morale boosting vary in organizations. Some companies have no dress code. Others provide an employee gym; some others provide a nap room. Some use no titles and no assigned parking places. Goldman Sacks in New York is reputed to give employees a limo ride home if they work late. These benefits may help you decide between two offers, or they may have no effect on your decision.

Whatever they are, these *perks* make employees believe they are important. Even if they are never used, the extras help build a strong morale. Ask your interviewer if his company has any such goodies! They may create a deeper engagement for you at the company, and engagement is what your employer, and you, will want. Too many people have little to no engagement at their place of employment. They come and go and typically don't last. If your company does any of the following, your engagement will deepen.

The Gallup company lists the 12 elements of employee engagement[1].

1. I know what is expected of me at work.
2. I have the materials and equipment I need to do my work right.
3. At work, I have the opportunity to do what I do best every day.
4. In the last seven days, I have received recognition or praise for doing good work.
5. My supervisor, or someone at work, seems to care about me as a person.
6. There is someone at work who encourages my development.
7. At work, my opinions seem to count.

---

[1] https://shrm.org/hr-today/news/hr-magazine/pages/0510fox3.aspx

8. The mission or purpose of my organization makes me feel my job is important.
9. My associates or fellow employees are committed to doing quality work.
10. I have a best friend at work.
11. In the last six months, someone at work has talked to me about my progress.
12. This last year, I have had opportunities at work to learn and grow.

Question 43

How Long Have You Been With the Company?

You should check the qualifications of the person who is interviewing you. Has this person been at the company long enough to know the answers to your important questions? What is the interviewer's point of view? Does this person convey happiness or satisfaction? Are they welcoming? Do these feelings seem to stem from job satisfaction?

The longevity of employees at a company can be an important indicator of the level of satisfaction employees experience working for that company. High turnover indicates something in that work environment causes employees to leave after a short period of time. That may be a red flag to you unless you can find the reason for the high turnover.

I am amazed at the timidity of most of the students who mock-interview with me or ask me questions about their pending interviews. They act as if they are powerless in the interview process. They would never dream of asking this question, and other questions to which they are entitled to answers.

You can ask this kind of question in a conversational, nonaggressive way. Interviewers should not find this question threatening; they should welcome it. Hey, this is your life we're talking about. These are your talents being recruited. These are your eight (10–12 or more) hours per day of labor. This is your second family. You need to know all you can about them.

According to a most recent Job Openings and Labor Turnover Survey (JOLTS) from the Bureau of Labor Statistics (BLS), over 3.5 million Americans quit their jobs every month, about 2.3 percent of the labor force.

According to LinkedIn's *2019* Workforce Learning Report, 94 percent of employees say that they would stay at a company longer if it simply invested in helping them learn and develop as employees[2].

---

[2] https://learning.linkedin.com/content/dam/me/business/en-us/amp/learning-solutions/images/workplace-learning-report-2019/pdf/workplace-learning report-2019.pdf

This interest in learning and development is particularly strong among younger workers. LinkedIn's research found that roughly a quarter of Gen Z and millennials say learning is the number one thing that makes them happy at work, and over a quarter (27 percent) of Gen Z and millennials say the number one reason they'd leave their job is because they did not have the opportunity to learn and grow.

And, there are signs that employers are beginning to catch on[3]. Savvy employers offer employee enrichment programs and tuition reimbursement to encourage employees to grow and develop. These are the organizations you want to work for.

---

[3] https://cnbc.com/2019/02/27/94percent-of-employees-would-stay-at-acompany-for-this-one-reason.html

SECTION 6

Ask About the Salary and the Selection Process

Question 44

How Many People Are You Interviewing for This Position?

Companies use recruiters and machines to make decisions related to filling positions. They search for key words and skills in cover letters and resumes and then choose a dozen or so people to interview. They know the number of people interviewing and the target start date for the position. When they share this number with you, they give you a sense of the competition and the timing of the process. You will want to know about both, the competition for the job and the timing, so do not be afraid to ask this and other questions related to the process, which are, in many respects, the most important questions you can ask.

The average number of people who apply for any job is 118, according to a *Forbes Magazine* article in 2017! That typically gets winnowed down to 25 or so, then to 10, maybe. After that, a handful will be offered a face-to-face interview. In any event, know how much competition you face.

Companion Questions to This One
  45. What is the process for selection of the final candidate?
  46. What is the salary range for this position?
  47. What is the benefit package and is it negotiable?
  48. How would you describe, in one word, working at this company?
  49. How did I do in this interview?
  50. When will I find out that I have been chosen?

Question 45

What Is the Process for Selection of the Final Candidate?

Your interviewer either will, or will not, have some kind of obvious process for selection (or will have a loose one floating around inside his/her cranium). I always asked human resources (HR) to provide 10 or 12 people for me to interview. Based on the results of those interviews, I created a *short list* of three or four. I then asked my staff to interview these finalists. From start to finish, the interview and selection process took 4 to 6 weeks. Added to the time it took to justify replacing or creating the position, placing the order with HR, placing the ad, collecting responses (usually 100–200), scanning 175, reading 25, setting up the interviews, interviewing, choosing a candidate, and making an offer (to be followed by the new person's two- to four-week notice at their current position).

After that, we might have given a test (a writing sample for a writer), done a background check, a reference check, and then made an offer in writing.

Companion Questions to This One

    44. How many people are you interviewing for this position?

    46. What is the salary range for this position?

    47. What is the benefit package and is it negotiable?

    48. How would you describe, in one word, working at this company?

    49. How did I do in this interview?

    50. When will I find out that I have been chosen?

Question 46

What Is the Salary Range For This Position?

Most employers have established a range of compensation for their positions. Let's say the range is $60,000 to $80,000. Many employers will also bring new people into the organization at the mid-point, in this case, $70,000. Many try to bring people in below the mid-point, especially so that they have a chance to receive salary increases in the position. By the way, if you are asked, "What are your salary requirements?" You should ask, in return, what is the salary range and then ask to be brought in at the mid-point. I tease my students and tell them to answer the question about salary requirements, "I have no upward limit!" Hey, even interviewers like a little humor to break the tension of an interview!

According to the Society for Human Resource Management (May 2018), "A traditional salary range is commonly 30 to 40 percent. It is common that top salary grades (i.e., for executives and top management) have a wider range (sometimes greater than a range of 40 percent), and that the lowest salary grades often have the narrowest range (sometimes smaller than 30 percent)[1].

Giving a new employee a salary too close to the top means giving yearly increases that quickly take the employee to the maximum salary range. That, of course, gives no incentive to work harder.

Companion Questions to This One
   44. How many people are you interviewing for this position?
   45. What is the process for selection of the final candidate?
   47. What is the benefit package, and is it negotiable?
   48. How would you describe, in one word, working at this company?
   49. How did I do in this interview?
   50. When will I find out that I have been chosen?

---

[1] https://shrm.org/resourcesandtools/tools-and-samples/how-to-guides/pages/howtoestablishsalaryranges.aspx#:~:text=A%20traditional%20salary%20range%20is,sometimes%20smaller%20than%2030%20percent)

Question 47

What Is the Benefit Package, and Is It Negotiable?

Many enlightened employers use the benefits package to recruit, as it is much more flexible than the salary schedule. You might negotiate more vacation, in lieu of the smaller salary. You might ask that your student loan be paid off. You might ask that your expected MBA studies be financed. You might ask for a four-day, 10-hour per day work schedule. Use your imagination!

To negotiate changes to the benefits package, make sure you pursue this in a manner that places you in the best position to get those benefits that matter most to you.

Review these *rules* from Harvard's Deepak Melhotra:

Don't underestimate the importance of likability. This sounds basic, but it's crucial: People are going to fight for you only if they like you.

Help them understand why you deserve what you're requesting. It's not enough for them to like you. They also have to believe you're worth the offer you want. Never let your proposal speak for itself—always tell the story that goes with it.

Make it clear they can get you. If you intend to negotiate for a better package, make it clear that you're serious about working for this employer.

Understand the person across the table. Companies don't negotiate; people do. And, before you can influence the person sitting opposite you, you have to understand them.

Understand their constraints. They may like you. They may think you deserve everything you want. But they still may not give it to you. Why? Because they may have certain ironclad constraints, such as salary caps, that no amount of negotiation can loosen.

Therefore, focus on benefits and nonsalary items such as repayment of student loan debt, travel expenses, rent subsidies, and so on.

Be prepared for tough questions. Before a company makes concessions, they want to know you are ready and willing to step into the position in their timeframe. Many job candidates have been hit with difficult questions they were hoping not to face: Do you have any other offers?

If we make you an offer tomorrow, will you say yes? Are we your top choice[2]?

Negotiation requires skill and attention. Be certain you are ready when you begin to negotiate.

Companion Questions to This One
    44. How many people are you interviewing for this position?
    45. What is the process for selection of the final candidate?
    46. What is the salary range for this position?
    48. How would you describe, in one word, working at this company?
    49. How did I do in this interview?
    50. When will I find out that I have been chosen?

---

[2] https://hbr.org/2014/04/15-rules-for-negotiating-a-job-offer

Question 48

How Would You Describe, in One Word, Working at This Company?

You will spend the rest of your life working (unless you hit the lottery or invent the next step in artificial intelligence). So, you should decide here and now to find work that satisfies and fulfills you. If your interviewer says that the place is *intense*, that's one thing. If she answers that the organization is *innovative*, that's quite another. Or, perhaps she'll say *collaborative*. That one word can make all the difference. Maybe, she'll say it's *fun* and she can't wait to get to work every day.

Should employees have fun at work? Absolutely. Look at this research from an article entitled, "Should employees have fun at work?"

1. **Having fun improves communication.** Research sponsored by Alfresco concludes that 65 percent of knowledge workers collaborate multiple times a day. Fun improves communication, and therefore, encouraging fun could be a great way to improve the quality of that collaboration.

2. **Having fun helps us learn better.** In a video interview with business psychologist Simon Kilpatrick, we learn that people learn better when they are having fun. So, if continuous improvement and development is important to a company and its brand, then that company should encourage fun at work.

3. **Having fun makes employees more productive.** According to research published by CIPHR, productivity is directly linked to happiness. And, when employees are having fun, they tend to be happier[3]. So, try to find an employer that encourages a positive, sometimes fun environment.

The bottom line is that you must ask this question to see what spontaneous, and usually accurate, answer you receive.

---

[3] https://peoplehr.com/blog/2018/05/30/should-employees-have-fun-atwork/#:~:text=So%20if%20continuous%20improvement%20and,they%20tend%20to%20be%20happier

Companion Questions to This One
44. How many people are you interviewing for this position?
45. What is the process for selection of the final candidate?
46. What is the salary range for this position?
47. What is the benefit package, and is it negotiable?
49. How did I do in this interview?
50. When will I find out that I have been chosen?

Question 49

How Did I Do in This Interview?

I always encourage students to ask, after the interview, "How did I do?" You are entitled to an answer, even though most will be unprepared to give you one. They will likely hem and haw before finally saying something noncommittal. So, why bother? You may find someone who gives you an honest answer. And, as always, you want to leave the session knowing the interviewer will remember you. Ask a difficult question, and this might happen.

Should an interviewer answer truthfully, you may gain valuable information that could improve your interviewing skills. You may rephrase the question to, "Do you have any suggestions to improve my interviewing?" Interviewing is a process, and as such, we can learn to improve our technique from those on the receiving end of our efforts. And, remember what one interviewer disliked, another may welcome. For example, an interviewer may say you were too aggressive. A sales position needs a certain amount of aggression and assertiveness. Say, thank you, and accept their feedback.

Companion Questions to This One
    44. How many people are you interviewing for this position?
    45. What is the process for selection of the final candidate?
    46. What is the salary range for this position?
    47. What is the benefit package, and is it negotiable?
    48. How would you describe, in one word, working at this company?
    50. When will I find out that I have been chosen?

Question 50

When Will I Find Out That I Have Been Chosen?

Notice that I didn't say, "If I have been chosen." You need to target the two or three places where you want to work and then do whatever is necessary to get a job there. Find out who interviews. Get to know them, if you can. Learn their needs and figure out how you can satisfy them. Go to the interview prepared and be confident. Ask questions. Help the interviewing process. Be enthusiastic. Be interesting. Be hard, no, be impossible to reject. See yourself in the job.

It may sound New Age, but I believe in positive visualization. I once asked for my interviewer's business card, and when I got home, I scratched out his name and printed mine in its place. I stared at that thing and repeated a mantra, "Ed Barr, Director of Corporate Communications." I got the job!

We don't always get the job we set out to get. But, sometimes, we end up getting a better job. Whatever the case, positive visualization and a positive attitude work in your favor.

Companion Questions to This One

    44. How many people are you interviewing for this position?

    45. What is the process for selection of the final candidate?

    46. What is the salary range for this position?

    47. What is the benefit package, and is it negotiable?

    48. How would you describe, in one word, working at this company?

    49. How did I do in this interview?

PART III

Exhibit Warmth and Competence

Asking and answering questions are, of course, the heart of the job interview. All job candidates fret over how they will answer tough questions. In many ways, answering the hardest questions is about *the way you answer them*, not necessarily what you answer. According to a *Harvard Business Review* article, employers are looking for two thing in an employee, warmth and competence[1].

I will add confidence to those.

Let's look at them one at a time. First, what does it mean when employers are looking for *warmth*? That's easy. They want to know if you will fit in with the team. They want to know if they'd enjoy working next to you, if they'd have a cup of coffee with you and enjoy it. We spend so much time at work and as part of a team that we need to coalesce. We need to collaborate. We need to get along and like each other. If we can't do that, if we can't trust each other, and things go awry, fixing it will be more challenging than for a well-functioning team. If you have warmth, you have emotional intelligence, too. You can empathize, listen, resolve conflict, solve problems, and so forth.

What does it mean to be competent? That varies, of course, from job to job, especially with technical jobs. When you interview, the organization wants to know simply if you can do your job. Will you work hard, and are you self-motivated? I was always looking for people who I had to chase, rather than those I had to jumpstart. I wanted people who were confident enough to try things and make mistakes. Of course, it helped if they had a record of successes.

---

[1] https://hbr.org/2015/05/how-to-show-trustworthiness-in-a-job-interview

So, when you are being interviewed, you need to reflect warmth, competence, and confidence. That has a direct bearing on how you answer interview questions. And, it all begins as you step into the interview room. It starts with your appearance, your attire, your body language. Do these reflect confidence, and are they built to create a great first impression?

Dress for Success

One of the most powerful influencers, according to the research of Robert Cialdini, is *liking*. We can be influenced by people who are like us. This takes many forms, and one obvious form is people who dress the same way we do. That means it's important to know how the people who are interviewing you dress for work. Do they wear suits or jeans and tee shirts? A friend who owns a business called on a start-up firm while wearing a suit and tie. He knew the moment he entered their offices that he would not get the work. The people he called on all wore jeans and tee shirts.

Make a Good First Impression

What first impression do you give? This is reflected in your posture, your eye contact, your smile, dress, and your overall bearing. When the interviewer decides that you are the image of the employee they are looking for, they will likely look to confirm their bias. That is, they will look for the reasons why you are the ideal person. The opposite can also happen; they will begin to look for the reasons why you are not the right candidate for the job.

That reminds me, when you enter the building where you are to interviewed, stand until you are greeted by someone, remain standing until they invite you to sit, stay eye-to-eye with them, not below them. You don't want them to look down on you. When the interview begins, be prepared to say something great. You might say, "I am so excited to have this opportunity." In any event, practice your opening and script it so that you'll have it memorized. The rule of *primacy and recency* says that the first thing you say and the last thing will be remembered. Make them memorable.

Answer Questions With Confidence

Even if you're unsure of the interview question, answer it with confidence. I had a music teacher who told me, "If you play it wrong, play it strong." In other words, if you make a mistake, appear as if you meant to do it. Don't vacillate. You also might say, with confidence, "I don't know that at this minute, but I will give you the answer before the end of the day." This is confidence in action, even when you don't know. Or, you may relate the question to an area in which you have competence. Lastly, in some cases, there are no right answers; there are only your answers. Say them with confidence, bravado, not arrogance, just confidence.

Tell Good Stories

Humans are storytellers. We can't avoid it. We tell stories all day. We evolved that way. We told stories about where game could be found. We told stories about our crops. We told stories about our ancestors. And, we still do. Everyone has stories. Think about the ones that you can tell in your interview, stories that illustrate your capabilities, your competence, and your ability to motivate and interact with others. When you do, you will be remembered. "Oh, that's the young woman who told us about the XYZ project." If you can't think of how to tell a story, use the STAR method—situation, task, action, and result. It might go something like this: "I was working Standard IT Services and my boss told me that we had an emergency deliverable for our most valuable client. We needed to give them a new security package in two days, a process that would usually take two weeks, minimum. She asked me to lead a team of four that I could put together and gave me a budget for overtime of $15K. I chose three of the best people, pulled them together, explained our situation, asked them for their input, and then we created a tight calendar. We finished the project on time and only used half of the allotted budget, The client was happy and the boss allowed us to split the $7500 among the four of us. I took $1500 and let the other three have $2K each."

Use the STAR System

The sharpest candidates use the STAR system to answer these questions and demonstrate their past successes. What is the STAR system? It's an acronym which stands for: situation, task, action, result. For example, here is an answer that I was given in an interview: "I was working at XYZ Company on a project with three other people (Situation). We had to complete a new billing system for ABC Company within two weeks (Task). At the end of the first week we were far from our goal because one of our team members was not doing his part. I spoke with him and learned that his mother was dying. We shifted much of his work to the rest of the team (Action). We finished the project one day ahead of schedule and were given a bonus. We gave the bonus to the employee whose mother passed away (Result)."

In summary, the best managers hire people who can function independently, with maturity and high ethical standards. They want employees who are not satisfied to complete only the work on their job description, but people who want to grow, experiment, and learn new skills. And, they want team players because they know that few great achievements result from the efforts of one person but by many in collaboration.

PART IV

How to Answer the Top 10 Hardest Questions You Will Be Asked

Check your local bookstore or Goggle and you will find plenty of books on how to answer tough questions at interviews. I offer you here, the best ways to answer the 10 hardest (nontechnical) questions. I base this on my many years of experience as a person who interviewed, and then offered jobs to many candidates. That said, let's take a look at the top 10.

The Top 10 Most Difficult Interview Questions

1. What Is Your Greatest Weakness?

We all have weaknesses. I don't attend to detail. I'm impulsive. I don't pay enough attention to budgets. I also don't speak Lithuanian. Do I work too hard? Most of the time. But, I'm not going to admit any of these as a weakness. If I am applying for a job in marketing management, I don't want to reveal the weaknesses I mentioned because they become true liabilities, deal breakers. I want to find a weakness that will do two things: (1) It will satisfy the questions and (2) It will be something that can be improved upon. Also, I don't want to use the trite "I work too hard."

So, what weaknesses are available? For my non-native students, I suggest they say, "I need to continue to improve my English language skills." For many students, I suggest they focus on a *soft skill* and say, perhaps, "I need to improve my communication skills (obviously this wouldn't work in a communication job)." If you're applying for a job in information technology (IT), maybe in coding, you don't want to say that a weakness is Python. However, we all know (stereotype coming) that IT people need to improve their soft skills.

HAVING A WEAKNESS IS OK, AS LONG AS YOU ARE WORKING TO IMPROVE IT

I put that in all-caps so that you will see it and remember it. If you say that your English language skills are suspect, you must tell the interviewer what you are doing to improve them. "I speak English with my American friends. I watch TV and listen to the ways they talk. I learn a new word every day." Remember, everyone has shortcomings, but not everyone works to improve them.

The Internet is teeming with advice on how to answer this question. Indeed.com tells you, "The key to preparing for this question is to identify weaknesses that still communicate strength. This will show the interviewer you're introspective enough to know your areas of opportunity"[1]. I think this is OK, but doesn't sound genuine. A Hub Spot message gives you these responses: "Patience when working with a team, Organization skills, Delegating responsibility, Can be too timid with my feedback, Can be too blunt with my feedback, Public speaking, and Analyzing data."[2] These sound like great liabilities in several jobs. But, again, your answer is not as important as the process you are using to improve. Whatever weakness you plan to acknowledge, show exactly the process you are using to improve.

2. Why Should We Hire You?

Remember this important advice, *THE INTERVIEW IS NOT ABOUT YOU; IT'S ABOUT THEM.*

I know, that sounds counterintuitive. But, really, they don't care so much about you as they do about WHAT YOU CAN DO FOR THEM. In answering any interview questions, talk about the benefits to them.

---

[1] https://indeed.com/career-advice/interviewing/list-of-example-weaknesses-for-interviewing

[2] https://blog.hubspot.com/marketing/what-is-your-greatest-weakness

Cite their objectives as a business and show them how you can help them achieve those objectives. Speak knowledgeably about them. For instance, when I hired marketing people, I wanted to hear them talk about how they would help us create innovative products, services, and solutions. I wanted them to speak with authority about our customers. I wanted them to give me ideas of how they would promote our products and services. They could connect that to work they had already done. But, tread cautiously in focusing on your previous efforts; the more they talked about themselves, the faster I become bored. Don't tell me what you did for someone else, tell me what you will do for me. This obviously requires more than a passing knowledge about the company you are interviewing with. Remember WIIFM!

3.Why Do You Want This Job?

This presents you with the perfect opportunity to tell them how great they are. It's that simple. "All of my colleagues would die to work here. You are the leader. Your reputation is second to none." Believe me, you can't say enough great things about them. We're all this way. We want to be loved. We want to be told how great we are. "I know that I will learn more here than I did in college. You have the best learning and develop-ment program. You are ranked third in the list of the best companies to work for" and on and on.

4.Tell Me What You Didn't Like About Your Last Job

People leave jobs mostly because they have bad managers. You don't want to say outright, "I hated my manager," but you can list a situation or two where better management would have led to better outcomes because, of course, you take great pride in your work. You might say, "I worked on a number of projects with different people and I benefited from their guidance and feedback. However, my manager didn't supervise most of those projects. When I worked on projects supervised by my boss, he failed to give feedback on areas of possible improvement. I appreciate and seek feedback because I want to improve and grow."

5.Tell Me About a Time Your Work Was Criticized.

No one does perfect work all the time. We all make mistakes, so this question isn't about the mistake, it's about how you handled and processed the criticism. You can admit to being pained when your work was criticized. But, it's not OK to become paralyzed. I was once asked to write an introduction for an annual report for a publicly traded company. When I took the draft to the chief financial officer, he told me it wasn't good, that it sounded too much like "PR talk, too fluffy." I knew immediately that he was correct, and I told him I would redraft it. I went to a quiet place and put myself in the mind of a finance person. I wrote the message as un-fluffy as I could, paying attention to language that spoke to finance people. I took the second draft to him, he made a few corrections, and he said, "This works." I felt great. I had learned and succeeded. I knew I wouldn't make that mistake again. When you are asked about being criticized, use the STAR method—explain the Situation, the Task, the Action, and the Result. Show how you learned and benefitted—how you maturely handled the situation.

6.What Has Been Your Greatest Accomplishment?

Here is your chance to tell a story, your greatest ally in communication. Your story can be about any accomplishment from any time in your life, but you must make it relate to the job at hand. I had a student tell me that she placed third in an international piano competition when she was interviewing for a job in finance. She told me that she practiced six hours a day until her fingers hurt. She told me that she was studying for her college exams at the same time and trying to stay on the honor roll. She told me that it was often cold in her apartment and in the practice suite. She painted a word picture for me that allowed me to feel the way she felt. Then she spoke about the competition itself, how nervous she was, how talented and accomplished the other competitors were. She put me on the piano bench alongside her. Then, to top it off, she told me how the experience prepared her for a life in finance with its many pressures and uncertainties. I was ready to hire her on the spot. You, too, can use any accomplishment, as long as you relate it to the position you are interviewing for. Tell a story!

7.Tell Me About a Time You Disagreed With Your Boss

Bosses aren't perfect, far from it. We all have times when we think he might be on the wrong track. The important thing about this question is what process you used to resolve the situation. I tell my students to focus first on the communication aspects of this situation. For example, a student might answer this way, "My boss wanted to use television to reach our audience and I knew that social media would work better. So, I asked if I could meet with him. I asked him why he thought television was the best approach. I listened. I asked further questions. I told him why I thought social media was a better medium to use and showed him some data. I suggested that television would be a good adjunct to social media. He agreed and we compromised." This question is really about protocol, respect, process, listening, communicating, and conflict resolution.

8.Why Have You Been Out of Work?

Everyone has moments of unemployment, gaps on their resume. I have had mine. In fact, an interviewer once told me that my resume looked "like a rollercoaster" because I had changed jobs so many times in a short span. There are periods in your life when you are finding what your dream job looks like or you are transitioning to another career. If you have moments of unemployment, or several job transitions in a short amount of time, answer honestly and explain that you are not willing to take any job just to have a job. Say that you are willing to wait for the right job and not to deprive someone else of a job that best suits them. You might even say that the job you are now interviewing for is your dream job, and that you were willing to wait for this interview, that you had planned your life with enough savings and some freelance work to wait for this one perfect opportunity to become available.

9.What Is Your Salary Expectation?

Answer this question by asking the salary range. Then, say that because of your education, skills, and experience (if you have them) suggest that you should be brought in above the midpoint. That means, if the salary range is $50K to $100K, you'd like to be brought in above $75K. Always remember that people take jobs for money, but they stay in jobs for non-financial reasons. Also, remember that you can negotiate nonsalary items that bring you additional income. You can ask for a signing bonus; you can ask for a six-month review; you can ask for a different title, tuition support, housing expenses, travel, parking, and any number of other things that the company may be willing to offer to get around the salary range or scales.

10. What Would You Do if You Knew You Only Had One Year to Live?

Now, you must talk about what truly matters in your life. You need to say that work is important to you, but your family is more important. Say that you'd want to spend more time with your family. Be honest, no matter how much you love a job, most people do not want to spend their final days focused on work.

A List of Behavioral Questions

(With a Few Trick Questions Thrown in)

I routinely mock interview students. When I do, I keep a list handy that includes questions beyond the common ones we have just discussed. It has many questions, some of them weird, some of them probing, many of them behavioral. Below you will find my list. Remember that you can find many sources on the Internet, with questions and suggested answers. I have found that the key is to answer in such a way that you show a benefit to the company you are interviewing with or show your ability to tell stories. Here's my list:

1. Tell me about yourself in three words.
2. Why should I NOT hire you?
3. What can you do for me that I can measure?
4. What do you value?
5. What did you like least about your last job?
6. Describe a difficult business problem and the way you handled it.
7. How do you approach things you really don't like to do?
8. Why did you choose to become a -----------?
9. Tell me about a time you said NO to someone.
10. What do you look for in a job?
11. Tell me about a time your work was criticized.
12. Tell me about a difficult person you worked with.
13. What makes you think you can handle this job?
14. I don't think you can do this. Disagree with me.
15. Do you ever lie?
16. Sell me this pen.
17. What kind of cartoon character would you be?
18. How many cats are there in NY City?
19. How would you divert a hurricane?
20. Tell me a good story.
21. What would you do if you knew you could not fail?
22. What could you talk about for 30 minutes with absolutely no preparation?
23. What question would you most like to know the answer to?

24. What would you do with the extra time if you didn't have to sleep?

25. What has been the most stressful moment of your life?

26. If you could invite anyone, living or dead, to dinner, who would it be?

27. If a crystal ball could tell you anything, what would you want to know?

28. What makes you feel most alive?

29. What do you regret not doing? Why haven't you done it?

30. What is something you know you do differently than other people?

PART V

Some Mock Interviews

Before venturing out on any interview, whether you have done this numerous times before or never before, you should prepare for the interview by doing mock interviews with friends, teachers, or colleagues. The following interviews resemble mock interviews that I have done over the years. Review them. Examine each to see if they become conversations, not a one-sided grilling. Does the candidate respond well and encourage a dialogue with appropriate questions? Does the candidate appear to be arrogant or contentious? Do the candidate and interviewer seem to be equals?

Interview # One

Follow along as we watch "Irma Candidate" interviewing with "Ray Recruiter." Judge for yourself if Irma exercises at least some control over this face-to-face interview by creating and maintaining a dialogue and conversation, using questions, in a confident and assertive, but not arrogant, manner.

RAY: Good day, Ms. Candidate. Thank you for agreeing to sit with me to discuss the position at our company.

IRMA: You are quite welcome Mr. Recruiter. I am thrilled to be here and I thank you for this excellent opportunity. (A broad smile here will help, along with any appropriate gestures and open body language. When you gesture, use open palms and keep your arms at the same width as your shoulders. Don't point with your index finger; instead, use your open hand to point. As for other body language, fold your hands at your chest when not gesturing and keep your arms and legs uncrossed. Sit parallel to the person interviewing you and use your face and voice to show enthusiasm and energy.)

RAY: Great. This should take no more than 45 minutes. I have some questions I'd like to ask and I expect that you have some questions you'd like to ask me. Does this work for you?

IRMA: It does. I'm looking forward to a great conversation.

RAY: Good. Well, tell me, may I call you Irma?

IRMA: Certainly.

RAY: Well, tell me, Irma, why do you want to work for us? (This is a common question.)

IRMA: Actually, there are many reasons, Mr. Recruiter.

RAY: Please call me Ray.

IRMA: Yes, Ray, as I said there are many reasons, but I'm just going to focus on three: your reputation in the industry, your record of promoting the growth and development of your employees, and the match I see between your needs and my skillset. (It's good to make answers concrete and, as a result, memorable.) As I have followed your company through the media and though your website, I have found your company to be one of the leaders in your field. You were named one of the 100 Best Firms to Work For last year, and your reputation for ethical practice is unmatched. Similarly, I have spoken with people who have worked for you, and they tell me that the opportunities for growth are excellent. When I match my skillset to the needs of your company, I see a perfect fit. Tell me, is this an accurate depiction of your company? Do you provide opportunities for employees to grow?

RAY: Absolutely, Irma. Whomever you spoke with told you the truth. Last year, for example, two of our executive positions were filled from internal promotions. I myself began here nine years ago in an entry-level position and now head my section. Our retention rate is over 80 percent.

IRMA: That's amazing, Ray. How would you describe the culture here? (This is becoming a conversation.)

RAY: We like to think that we are collaborative, exciting, fast-paced and family-oriented. We work mostly in self-directed teams. We allow people to make mistakes, and we give people a chance to excel. Let me ask you, Irma, what do you believe has been your greatest work-related achievement to date?

IRMA: I was fortunate to work on a team of four people at my last job. (Here Irma can use the STAR system—situation, task, action, result.) We were working with a long-time customer who tasked us with creating a new billing function for their large non-profit organization, and we were given only two weeks to complete the project. After the first week, we were woefully behind, so I gathered the group together and we talked openly about the situation. One of the members was not keeping up, and we discovered that he had no idea how to code his part of the project but didn't want to admit it. We swapped roles and gave him a task that he could excel at, and we finished that project two days ahead of schedule. The client was happy, our boss was happy, and we were given a small bonus, which we used to have dinner together. It was a win–win for everyone. I feel very comfortable working in teams and feel that, when run efficiently, they can benefit companies. Does your company use teams to work on projects, Ray?

RAY: As I mentioned earlier, we also use self-directed teams, Irma. Very few projects are handled by an individual. Can you tell me how you communicated with your team and your boss during those two weeks?

IRMA: Two of the team members were remote, so we used Zoom with regular meetings scheduled every day. I took a leadership role in that by creating agendas, sending them ahead of our meetings, and sending the links. With two people in Asia, we had to schedule carefully because of the time difference. We set ground rules before we began that asked us each to pledge to be open to suggestions and committed to results. That's how we found the problems. The team was using Google Hangouts and a company website where we could look at each other's work. We agreed upfront to trust each other. I sent my boss daily e-mail updates, and we had agreed to meet twice during the week to discuss the project. She was readily accessible and supportive and that made things much easier for the team and me.

It was a true team success. Would you describe the management style of this company as accessible and supportive, Ray?

RAY: Absolutely, Irma.

Review

If you study this interaction carefully, you will see two people in an easy conversation, both contributing and revealing essential aspects important to each other. Irma, the candidate, has tagged on comments made by Ray the recruiter to ask important and timely questions about the company. Ray has used the same opportunities to learn about Irma and her potential as a future employee.

Interview # Two

In this setting, we find "Carl Candidate" and Marilyn Manager" as they begin an interview. Judge for yourself if Carl exercises some control over this interview by creating and maintaining a dialogue and conversation, using questions, in a confident and assertive, but not arrogant, manner.

MARILYN: Please have a seat, Mr. Candidate (she points to a chair in front of her desk and he sits). Thank you for coming today. Have you brought a copy of your resume (he hands her a copy)? Thank you. I trust you had no trouble finding this office.

CARL: Your directions were very clear. I've been interested in your company for some time and know that you also have offices in India. Does this position involve any travel?

MARILYN: It may, Mr. Candidate, and we will come to that. But, for now, tell me a little about yourself.

CARL: You may call me Carl. I am a resourceful person, Ms. Manager. (Carl now has a chance to tell a story and create a memory for the interviewer.) Just to give you an idea, I was waiting for an important telephone call one evening and I noticed that my cell phone battery was low, so I decided to charge it. When I tried to use the charger, it wasn't working.

I didn't have a landline, it was late, and I was living by myself, so I had to improvise. As it happened, I had some spare parts laying around, so I built a charger and was able to take the call. I have always been able to find ways to get things done, especially under difficult circumstances. Is this a characteristic that is valued at this company?

MARILYN: Yes, it certainly is, Carl. We value innovation, as you would have noted on our website. Can you walk me through your resume?

CARL: Absolutely. As you probably saw from the resume that I submitted through your hiring portal, I have the best education from one of the best universities in the world, Carnegie Mellon University, and I have had work experience at one of the best companies. But, I'd like to direct you to the special interest section at the bottom of my resume where you will see that I have had much involvement with the "Hunger Project," a global effort to feed starving children. (Carl now has another chance to tell a memorable story.) I was traveling in India when I saw a child putting stones in his mouth. I asked our tour guide why he was doing that, and she said because he is hungry and has no food. She said that, often, the children swallow the stones. That made a lasting impression on me, and I vowed to help in some small way to bring food to those kinds of children. I was excited to see that your company supports efforts in the Third World. How are employees encouraged to participate?

MARILYN: We have a management-by-objectives system, and all employees are required to write yearly goals, one of which is a "values goal." You would have seen these values on our website. Did you?

CARL: I did. As I recall, they include integrity, community, excellence, innovation, and fair return on equity. Am I correct?

MARILYN: Very good, Carl. Actually, the last one is "fair return to our investors," but you obviously came prepared. So, what would your last employer say about you?

CARL: I'm glad you asked that. I had a very positive experience at my last company and left under the best terms. I'm sure when you contact them, they will say that I was a great employee, one who always finished his work on time and was an enthusiastic team player, a person who went out of his way to find the work that needed to be done and then created plans for accomplishing that work. May I ask you what the culture is like at this company?

Review

Here, again, you see two people in conversation. This conversation takes a much different route from the first interview but achieves many of the same goals. Interviewer and candidate learn about one another and each sees how they fit together.

Interview # Three

Follow along as this interview unfolds. Does this sound like a conversation? Does it flow smoothly? Here we find Rhonda Recruiter interviewing Colin Candidate.

RHONDA: Welcome, Mr. Candidate. May I get you a drink of water?

COLIN: No, thanks.

RHONDA: Well, let's begin then. Can you tell me how you learned about this position?

COLIN: I saw it posted on LinkedIn.

RHONDA: What interested you in the position?

COLIN: I admire your company and think I can do a good job for you.

RHONDA: What makes you think you can do a good job?

COLIN: I have studied Python, C++, and "R." I have two years of coding experience.

RHONDA: Can you tell me about a time when you used Python on a project?

COLIN: As you know, Python is a scripting language for Web applications. It can automate specific series of tasks, and it's very efficient. I used it on a software application at the company where I worked, for some pages within a Web browser.

RHONDA: What do you do when you're not coding?

COLIN: I like to play video games.

Review

As anyone can observe, this seesaw rocks back and forth until the recruiter ends the pain. This is not a conversation, not a dialogue. It's an interrogation. Many recruiters are probably accustomed to this kind of interaction because it's all too common. It makes for a very boring experience for both people and doesn't dig under the surface to find the deeper aspects of either the job or the candidate. It's unilateral, a one-sided event. Additionally, I would guess that the candidate is failing to make good eye contact or use gestures and body language to keep the interviewer engaged.

In this interview, perhaps something happened to the candidate before the interview that is impacting his performance. Perhaps he showed up late for the interview because a massive wreck brought traffic to a stand-still for 30 minutes. Even though he phoned ahead to let the interviewer know he would be late and why, when he arrives, he knows this is not the best way for an interview to begin. But, he can turn this around. He needs to take a few deep breaths, focus on the interview, and be confident in his ability to re-engage the interviewer with more detailed answers and appropriate questions.

Interview # Four

In some interviews, recruiters ask trick questions. When you encounter a trick question, keep this in mind: the answer to the question is not as important as your reaction and thinking process. Follow this next interview and watch what happens.

TRICKY RICKY RECRUITER:	All right, Colleen, you've been doing very well so far. Now I have a question that will engage your mind more deeply. How many dogs are there in New York City?
COOL COLLEEN:	That's an interesting question. Before I answer, can I ask some clarifying questions?
TRICKY RICKY RECRUITER:	Of course. Shoot!
COOL COLLEEN:	Are you talking about Manhattan or all five boroughs?
TRICKY RICKY RECRUITER:	All boroughs.
COOL COLLEEN:	If I'm not mistaken, the population is just over eight million people. Does that sound correct to you?
TRICKY RICKY RECRUITER:	Yep, that sounds about right.
COOL COLLEEN:	Well, let's assume that of those eight million people, half of them are part of families (that's four million) and let's assume that half of those families have pets (that's two million). If that's true, perhaps half of those have dogs; that leaves things at one million. If my math is correct, I'd say that by subtracting some, the number of dogs would come to around 750,000. (Actually, according to *The NY Times*, there are 500,000 dogs in NY City.)

Review

What makes Colleen a success here? It's her calm and her thinking process. As we see, she has overestimated the number of dogs by a quarter million, but she responded with the kind of control that a company would want any staff to exhibit. Trick questions have become common in many interviews, as have technical questions, especially for technical candidates.

I have coached students who have been asked technical questions that they should have known but totally blanked on. I tell them to say, "I don't know the answer this minute but if you give me an hour I will have that answer for you." No one has all the answers all the time; recruiters know this. We want people who can think under pressure, people who are resourceful, people who don't fluster easily.

Interview # Five

These days, everyone conducts *behavioral interviews* and for good reason. They help us understand how people have behaved in the past or will behave under certain circumstances in the future. Follow along here to watch a behavioral interview unfold and think about how the candidate answered the questions or should have answered them. Also, see how the recruiter has used questions to keep the conversation going.

QUINN QUESTIONS: Thanks for coming in today to be interviewed, Mr. Bigg. We like your resume, especially your work experience, and we wanted to get to know you a little better. Think of this as a behavioral interview with a series of behavioral questions.

BOBBY BIGG: Thank you. I'm delighted that you called me back for this second round. I'm anxious to show you that I'm the person best qualified to fill this important position for you.

QUINN QUESTIONS: All right, let's get started then. Can you tell me about a time when you disagreed with your boss, and what actions you took to resolve that disagreement?

BOBBY BIGG: Well, this has actually never happened to me, but, if it did, I would do a few things. First, I would ask for a meeting with her to try to understand her point of view. I'd try to make sure we were defining terms the same way. Mostly I would listen. If I felt that she was in error, I would try to show her how a different decision would benefit her and the organization. People disagree often and even when they have the same ends in mind. Communication is critical in today's complex organizations, including, I am sure, yours. Is this the kind of approach you believe will work at this company?

QUINN QUESTIONER: Yes, we constantly strive to perfect our communications, both internally and externally. In fact, we have a series of classes through HR where we invite industry experts in communication to help us improve. But, let's explore another question. Can you tell me about a project that you worked on that did not achieve the desired goals?

BOBBY BIGG: Yes, I can. A few years ago, back in my undergraduate days, I was working with a team of six people on a capstone project. We had one of the big consulting firms as a client, and they wanted us to help them to better utilize their extensive customer database. We worked on that project for six weeks, and I'm unhappy to say that it was mostly a failure. As I reflect on it, I put the failure in my hands as the team leader. It had many moving parts, and I was not mature enough as a businessperson to understand. I also let my ego get in the way. But, I learned so much from it. Our primary contact was in another city, and that person was mostly inaccessible to me. Then, in the middle of the project, he left the company. I didn't understand the necessity for intense communication with the client or for me to step up and assert myself. I was thinking too much like a college student. I also let the team members drift from their responsibilities. I learned that we needed to write our responsibilities on a contract and sign it. I learned that I needed to act like a leader by regularly interacting with everyone involved, especially the client. Ultimately, the client accepted the blame, but I knew that I could have done better. Ironically, our advisor gave us an "A" on the project, knowing that the project was compromised when the client left the company, but I still consider it both a small failure and a big learning experience. How are failures looked upon at this company?

QUINN QUESTIONER: We encourage innovation, and no one is punished for failing when they have done as much as they could to succeed. You say you "let your ego get in the way." What did you mean by that?

BOBBY BIGG: I wanted to be perceived as THE leader, but I didn't fully understand what leadership means. I have since learned that a leader empowers others and creates transparency, a leader serves others, and motivates them. A leader also provides continuous feedback. After two years of work experience, I now feel that I can lead. With a more mature understanding of what that means. Does this position require leadership skills?

QUINN QUESTIONER: Yes, it does, Bobby. Tell me about a time you said "no" to someone.

BOBBY BIGG: Certainly. I was out with some friends for a bachelor party, and they wanted to keep pouring liquor into our friend who was going to get married the next day. I told them it was a bad idea, and that he would suffer from a hangover and certainly not enjoy what was meant to be one of the best days of his life. It took lots of persuasion, but they finally agreed with me, and we took him home while he was still in decent shape.

Review

You will note that Bobby has never disagreed with his boss but that does not prevent him from answering this behavioral question. Many people who interview have not had the breadth of experiences that others have had, but they can imagine what would happen and how they would behave. That answer is as satisfactory as another. You will also see that Bobby calls close attention to a time when he failed by letting his ego "get in the way." We all have egos and the desire to be recognized for doing good work. We like titles, such as *team lead*, or *project coordinator*, and if we're not careful, we forget what leadership means. We will all fail at one time or another in our work, but we succeed when we learn from our failures. Bobby is showing this recruiter that he has learned. Lastly, Bobby has used a personal story to tell about a time when he took control of a situation and said, "no." He demonstrated that by taking control of a situation, he helped it come to a better conclusion. Again, we don't all have a great depth of work experience, but we all have life experiences that translate into potential work performance. We can use them to show our behavior.

Storytelling

We've mentioned this before: Interviewing is not unlike storytelling. You are telling true stories about yourself to help another person better understand you and your talents and differentiation. How do you tell a good story? According to mythologist, Joseph Campbell, the hero sets out on a path with a goal, meets obstacles along the way, undergoes tension and conflict, and finally, resolves them to achieve a goal and come to a new realization[1]. If you review the mock interviews previously mentioned, you

---

[1] https://en.wikipedia.org/wiki/Hero%27s_journey

will see this kind of storytelling. Stories are powerful means to create understanding and long memory. You may hear storytelling referred to as *personal narrative* (tell me about yourself), or *STAR* (situation, task, action, result), or, perhaps, even *elevator pitch*.

What Animal Would You Be?

Often in behavioral interviews, candidates get questions such as, "What animal would you be?" or, "If you were a color, which one would it be?" or, "If you were a movie star, which one would you be?" I have asked questions like this. In fact, I once interviewed candidates for the position of *Director of Community Affairs*, a position that required building relationships between our organization and many diverse community groups, each with its own interests. It was a position that required the greatest tact and sensitivity, as well as the ability to listen deeply and to encourage honest, and sometimes painful, dialogue. I had two final candidates and was interviewing each for the final time. I had a feeling that one of them was likely to be a little too aggressive for the position. I asked them both, in separate interviews, "What animal would you be?" One candidate said, "A bear. Sometimes I need to get what I need to get." That answer differed from the other candidate who said, "A dolphin. I like to lead, but I have a playful demeanor." Was this a scientific approach? Not really. But, often when we allow our nonconscious minds to surface our deepest thoughts, we reveal our core characters. I hired the dolphin, and the dolphin was perfect in the position, staying in the organization for 10 years and going on to lead a nonprofit community welfare agency.

The Rule of Primacy and Recency

This rule says that we remember the first things we hear and the last. Everything else drops into a trough of memory somewhere in the middle. This tells you that the first thing you say at an interview and the last thing you say will likely be remembered after you have left. If it's true, and research has shown that it is, you must prepare carefully for the first and last things you say at an interview. I've already suggested that you begin by saying, "I'm so excited to be here." That sets the mood for the interview.

As mentioned previously, storytelling is powerful. I would suggest that you then first try to tell a story. We live our lives by storytelling. We do it at the movies, on TV, in the news, in songs, and in many other ways. People even use tattoos to tell stories on their skin. Stories are alluring and powerful and, mostly, memorable. Try to tell a story in the beginning and at the end. However, make that story meaningful to the topic at hand. I had a student who grew up in Taiwan in a small village that was destroyed by an earthquake. His home was destroyed, along with his parents' business, and the family was displaced to a refugee camp. He was able to overcome that nightmare existence to be one of the top students in the makeshift school, to be accepted at a leading university, to be among the top students, and to be accepted into one of the most demanding programs at Carnegie Melon University in America. He was able to say that he is adaptable, resourceful, and focused—three qualities that fit perfectly into the jobs for which he was applying. Before we discussed storytelling, he had no idea that his personal story could help to make him memorable and differentiated.

Differentiation

More and more these days, the people who are interviewing for the same jobs that you want all have similar experience and credentials. You must find a way to differentiate yourself from them in a positive way.

Harvard's guru of strategy, Michael Porter, said that businesses have only three strategies to choose from: cost leadership (low or high cost), focus (or niche), and differentiation[2]. I believe that all three of his strategies reflect only one, differentiation. Let's face it; if you are low cost (like Walmart), you are differentiating yourself, and if you sell only harmonicas (like Hohner), you are in a niched, focused space, and you are also clearly differentiated.

So, back to interviewing, when you interview, you must be able to show what value you can add to the employer that the others cannot. This can amount to almost anything, from your professional or personal life.

---

[2] http://quickmba.com/strategy/generic.shtml

My student who survived an earthquake was able to tell a story that few could tell. That story revealed his strengths and differentiated him. I had a student who served in the South Korean Army (mandatory) and became an officer assigned to be the liaison officer to a general, both of them stationed near the border with North Korea. He was obviously able to talk about decision making under pressure, as well as chain of command. I had a student who was a concert pianist and placed third in an international piano competition. She was looking for a job in finance and wondered how that concert experience could help her in finance. She realized that her attention to detail (musical notes), her grace under tremendous pressure, and her years of dedication could all resonate with potential employers. And, it did. I followed through with these three students (and many others), and they told me that they had used their stories to positive effect in their interviews. The last student had a video of her performance to share with recruiters!

First Impressions

"You never get a second chance to make a good first impression," as the saying goes. It's true. We make decisions about people in a matter of seconds; some studies have suggested 27 seconds. Usually, too, you make this impression before you say a word[3]! If this is true, and we have evidence to prove that it is, you must be very careful about the first impression you make.

In general, you need to appear confident, not cocky but confident. How do you do that? You have a good posture with your shoulders back and your chin level, you have a smile, and you are making eye contact, not staring, but connecting with the other person and then looking away to let them look you over. Additionally, you are dressed appropriately and you smell good, from your breathe to your body.

---

[3] https://inc.com/peter-economy/according-to-this-truly-surprising-new-study-you-have-just-27-seconds-to-make-a-first-impression.html

Confirmation Bias

We make judgments about each other very quickly, and then, we try to prove to ourselves that these judgments are correct. It's called *confirmation bias*. If I judge you to be safe and useful in my world, then I am going to look for evidence to support that opinion and ignore evidence to the contrary. This means that it's critical for you to make that good first impression so that the person in front of you will seek evidence to confirm that good feeling. If the opposite happens, you will have to work very, very hard to change the bad impression.

PART VI

A Case Study

Teddy, 44, has been working for 13 years as a middle manager at a large health care organization in a mid-sized city. Making an average salary, he supports two children whom his wife is homeschooling. Although Teddy began his career as a schoolteacher, he became interested in marketing and took some classes to transition out of education and into a small marketing role at a community hospital in his hometown. Gaining a few years of experience, he left that position for a bigger role in a bigger city. Taking an entry-level position, he quickly became the director of the department. But now, he feels that he has no chance to move up in his current organization and has been looking at outside employment opportunities.

One day, Teddy spots an announcement for a vice president of marketing at a competing health care system, Tri-state Healthcare, also a not-for-profit. However, Tri-State Healthcare has been growing quickly by purchasing several hospitals and a medical school in another distant larger city. They are pursuing this strategy to compete with another large health care system in town, Mega Healthcare, which already owns a medical school and is aggressively buying local suburban hospitals. Media accounts taut Tri-State Healthcare's purchases in the distant town as the path to successfully compete with Mega Healthcare system. Teddy sees this job as an opportunity to get in on the ground floor of a massive successful health care system. He has been working at a not-for-profit organization with a mission focused on serving the poor.

The executive position with Tri-State Healthcare has a reputation as an aggressive *player*, one that has a big advertising budget, a creative director on staff, and all the markings of a for-profit. The opportunity really appeals to Teddy. He wanted to become a top executive; he'd like to make more money (and this job doubles his current salary), and he is looking for a change. This is happening at a time when hospitals in America, especially not-for-profits, are undergoing significant change, with a move away from independent hospitals to large hospital systems that are acquiring not just other hospitals but entire medical practices.

On the outside, the opportunity looks too good to be true to Teddy. He gets the interview, and he gets the job offer. He sees his experience valued, and he sees himself with the Vice President title on his business cards. More than that, however, he sees the big salary. He sees little else. Meanwhile, and unknown to Teddy, in its aggressive growth mode, the company he now plans to join has been operating in the red, losing millions while acquiring doctors' practices (the division Teddy will work for).

The CEO of Tri-State Health has been diverting millions of dollars from the endowment restricted to the main hospital of the system to save the floundering hospitals in the market where he purchased the medical school and other hospitals. Eventually, the losses and inappropriate diversion of funds become public and hundreds lose their jobs, including Teddy. And, various members of the administrative staff, including the CEO, go on trial for their inappropriate practices. But, that doesn't change the fact that Teddy lost his dream job because he was unaware he was being hired by an institution crashing into bankruptcy.

Some Questions to Ponder

What facts suggest Teddy's ultimate decision?

If you are Teddy, what do you do?

Why would you make the decision you are making?

Would the financial status of Tri-State Healthcare have deterred you from taking the position?

How important is a title?

Is it better to take a job temporarily to get an executive position to set you up for another executive position?

PART VII

Remember These Fundamental Truths About Interviewing

A Good Interview Is a Conversation

If you have an interview and one person does all the talking, it will be a failure. A good interview has two people in dialogue, in a conversation, learning about each other. It's not antagonistic and not investigative. It's natural discourse. If you talk too much, you'll bore the interviewer. If she talks too much, you can bet you're not going to get the offer. To have a good conversation, you need to listen and ask questions. You need to paraphrase, use body language to show that you understand, give feedback, in other words, use all the listening skills you have learned over the years. This is your first step in building a relationship, one that could last many years

You Are There to Interview Them

You are not a piece of property. You are a person who brings skills and talents to an organization, typically skills and talents that they need. Because we live in a world that provides service, for the most part, a service industry, the valuable commodity is not iron or steel, but people. Take the faculty and staff out of the university, for instance, and all you have left are buildings. Don't sell yourself short. Stay out of your own way. Decide where you want to take your skills and talents. Interview the interviewer.

First Impressions Are Critical

Yes, this advice bears repeating. "You never get a second chance to make a good first impression." I agree with that, in part. Certainly, if you make a bad first impression, you will have your work cut out for you to create a strong second impression. It does happen, but why go through all the trouble. Dress correctly. Groom well. Arrive early, don't rush in late. Have an erect posture. Have a big smile. Offer a firm handshake. Lean toward the interviewer. Mirror her when possible, and do it subtly. Use the power of your voice to enhance your enthusiasm. Make confident statements. Make it difficult for them not to hire you.

Storytelling Is Powerful

This may be the most important advice I can give you, so, yes, it also bears repeating. We live our lives by stories. We are told stories about the day when we were born, our first steps, our first day of school. You begin to accumulate stories of elementary school, middle school, and high school. Along the way, you learn the stories of your parents and grandparents, aunts and uncles. You see movies, read books, listen to music—all in the form of stories. Be ready to use this power when you are interviewed. Research has proven that we remember information when it's part of a story. We also mirror the storyteller and the characters in the story. I have asked hundreds of students to tell me their stories and then use them in an interview. It works.

Body Language Speaks Volumes

You don't have to say a word to communicate in an interview. Your nonverbal language will say it all. Your hairstyle, your clothes, your gestures—they all speak for you, even your shoes. Mostly, they communicate without your knowledge or the conscious knowledge of the person interviewing you. "The eyes are the windows of the soul," said Shakespeare. It's true. If you make too little eye contact or stare too deeply, you send a message. Your face has over 40 muscles, and it creates micro expressions you are not aware of. You can be communicating disgust or fear or sadness and not know it. Your hands, your arms, your legs—these also communicate.

One researcher said that, in an emotional situation, we only communicate with words 7 percent of the time. He added tone of voice accounting for 38 percent and body language at 55 percent. Many people have misinterpreted this research. Mehrabian has said, "Please note that this and other equations regarding relative importance of verbal and nonverbal messages were derived from experiments dealing with communications of feelings and attitudes (i.e., like-dislike). Unless a communicator is talking about their feelings or attitudes, these equations are not applicable[1]."

In any event, you show nervousness by crossing your arms over your heart, crossing your legs over you lap, blinking rapidly, or having a quaver in your voice.

You Must Differentiate Yourself

Anyone who applies for the same job you're after probably has very similar credentials. So, why should someone hire you? What can you do for us that the others cannot do? Perhaps you come from China but you speak and write both English and French fluently. You know that this international company is doing business globally, and you have traveled the world, backpacking and staying in hostels. In fact, once you were backpacking in northern India, near the Himalaya Mountain range when you lost your wallet, passport, and all identification.

Fortunately, you came upon a village where a French doctor was treating lepers. You were able to communicate through him and get supplies to retrace your steps and find your wallet. Do you see how you can combine storytelling with differentiation?

There Is No Perfect Job

And finally, there is no perfect job. Like every other aspect of our lives, perfection does not exist in jobs, either. There will always be some part of our jobs that we would like to change. So, we must ask ourselves, "Does this job, in general, give me satisfaction. Or is this job making my life miserable."

---

[1] https://eiagroup.com/communication-formula/

And, at different points in our careers, different jobs suit different lifestyles. In our youth, we may be willing to work long hours to establish and promote our career. Later in life, we may want to spend more time with a partner and a family. Those long hours at the office are no longer reasonable as we adjust to changing demands on our time. A long commute that seemed manageable becomes overwhelming after years of doing it. We may decide we no longer wish to work in the hustle and bustle of a city. Perhaps 70 percent of our job was travel, maybe we want to spend more time at home to be close to aging relatives or an ailing friend.

In conclusion, the dream job of our youth may cease to be that as we age. We must be honest with ourselves about what matters in a job and try to find a job that meets those needs. And, as we are honest with ourselves, we must be honest with our employer. Perhaps, given our changing needs, our employer can make adjustments to our work schedule or maybe offer a new position. But if that cannot happen, you need to consider finding another position. You may be older, but you bring with you years of varied experiences that can benefit a new employer. Don't sell yourself short, tell the employer what you can bring to their organization. Savvy employers understand and value experience.

PART VIII

Interviewing By Zoom and Other Virtual Technologies

Video Interviewing

In 2020, the world went remote. Most interviews went remote. Zoom came practically out of nowhere to lead the pack of virtual technologies. Suddenly, everyone was preparing for their Zoom interviews.

Whether the interview takes place on Zoom, Skype, Google Hangouts, or another platform, it's definitely not face-to-face. It's a very different experience. You need to use all of the techniques we've discussed so far, the conversation, the right attitude, the body language, tone of voice, and so on. But, some things you need to emphasize more than the others, such as background.

Give Your Background Depth

With face-to-face, you didn't have to worry about what your background looked like. It was provided. But, with virtual interviews, you need to arrange your background. In this virtual reality, many people are getting *Zoom Fatigue*. They experience it for several reasons, one of which is related to kinesthesia, our awareness of our physical position in relation to others. When we talk with someone in Zoom who is against a plain, flat background, we fatigue more easily. It has to do with our brains. Our brain gets upset if it can't put us in a three-dimensional space. It's also called proprioception. You will help the interviewer if you use dimension such as a room that has furniture in the background, a painting or photo, and anything else that gives you depth. The fatigue is happening non-consciously, but it's happening. So, address it.

Limit Movement Behind You

Movement attracts our attention. Our brains notice movement to keep us alive. If you have another person in your room and that person (or animal) enters the picture for any reason, you will lose the interviewer's attention. I once mock interviewed a student whose boyfriend kept walking in the background in and out of the room, shirtless. Needless to say, it was distracting. Disorder in the room also distracts us. So, straighten out your room; look neat.

Keep Your Camera at Eye Level

Any time you are being photographed, don't let the camera look up your nose. Don't *look up to* the interviewer and don't *look down on* her. Be at an even level with the interviewer and see her eye to eye.

Assume an Erect Posture

When you are not seated face-to-face with another person, it's easy to slump, to get too relaxed, especially if you're sitting in the comfort of your den in your pajama bottoms (another thing you shouldn't do). The military services speak of *command posture* for a reason. When you stand or sit upright with your shoulders back and your head erect, you have that posture and you exude a certain confidence.

Light Your Face and Upper Body to Best Effect

Don't keep yourself in the dark. Turn your camera so that you are looking out a window. You will likely achieve the Northern Light effect, a soft and flattering illumination. Whatever you do, don't put the light below your chin. If you do this, you will look like a devil. Check out the photo of

Germany's World War Two arms manufacturer, Alfred Krupp, as photographed by Arnold Newman. You will see the devil incarnate[1].

Use Your Eyes to Their Fullest Effect

When you interview virtually, you are essentially on television and you are an actor. The best actors use their eyes and faces to communicate, especially in extreme close-ups. If virtual interviewing is anything, it's the same kind of close-up. Make eye contact; look into the camera, not down or sideways.

Gesture the Right Way

When you're on video, you can use your hands to punctuate the points you're making but don't extend them beyond the camera. You will foreshorten them and make them look huge. If you decide to sit in the middle of the frame, a little further back from the camera, you will be able to gesture naturally but give up some eye contact. You objective is to animate yourself with every tool at your disposal. Organizations want to hire energetic, enthusiastic individuals, not mannequins.

Practice, tape yourself, know how you look, and improve that image.

Use the Power of Your Voice

When you interview through a device, you need to use your voice to its fullest advantage. You can use volume, tone, pitch, rate, and fluency

---

[1] https://google.com/search?ei=PUu4X6DSDKap5wKHx52ABw&q=krup
p+photo&oq=krupp+photo&gs_lcp=CgZwc3ktYWIQARgAMgUIABDJA-
zIGCAAQFhAeMgYIABAWEB4yBggAEBYQHjIGCAAQFhAeMgYIABAW
EB4yBggAEBYQHjIGCAAQFhAeMggIABAWEAoQHjIGCAAQFhAeO-
hEILhCxAxCDARDHARCjAhCTAjoFCC4QsQM6AgguOggILhDHARC-
vAToICC4QsQMQgwE6AggAOgUIABCRAjoFCC4QkQI6CwguELEDEM-
cBEKMCOggIABCxAxCDAToICAAQyQMQkQI6BQgAELEDOhEILh-
CxAxDHARCvARDJAxCTAjoOCC4QxwEQrwEQyQMQkwI6BAgAE-
ApQhzpYm2tgrXxoAXAAeACAAX6IAZsIkgEDNy40mAEAoAEBqgEHZ3dz
LXdperABAMABAQ&sclient=psy-ab

to speak with enthusiasm and energy. Use resonance; speak in the lower pitches. If you're a woman, try to lower your voice. We are impressed by low voices, probably because of evolution. When we heard low rumbles, either from storm clouds or the growls of wild animals, we paid attention. British Prime Minister Margaret Thatcher used a voice coach to help lower her voice so that she'd be taken more seriously. You can use a high pitch. When you are excited, your voice will probably rise in pitch. Try saying, "I just won the Powerball lottery" in a low-pitched voice. It's the same with rate and fluency. If you just won $300 million, you will probably tell people the news at a high rate of speed and with less fluency than if you were saying that your best friend was just hurt in an automobile accident.

Automated Interviewing

These days, we may never meet our interviewer, on video or face-to-face. Many interviews are recorded to be watched later by unknown persons. These interviews are called *automated* or *on demand* and consist of prerecorded questions. You are asked a question, given a short time to prepare an answer, and then the machine prompts you to answer the question while you're taped.

The finance industry and others have been using this technique. As reported on Monster.com, "...companies see this automated interview step as a way to make the hiring process more efficient. 'Scheduling interviews and going back and forth about availability takes up a lot of time,' says Rick Jordan, head of talent acquisition at Zappos, which also uses this method. 'Video interviewing is extremely flexible and convenient for the candidate. In fact, most responses came after 5 p.m. or on the weekends[2].'"

Check Your Equipment

If you know you will be interviewed in this way, obviously you must make sure your Internet connection is working, as well as your computer. You want speed and clarity so that your technology can help you look and sound your best.

---

[2] https://monster.com/career-advice/article/ace-recorded-job-interview-0916

Remember posture, eye contact, lighting, environment, and other critical factors.

Just as with a video interview on Zoom or other *computer face-to-face apps*, you must pay attention to your body language and non-verbal language. Even if there's no person in front of you, you must imagine there is. Eventually, a human watches your recording and makes judgments about you based on your posture, eye contact, and so on. Record in your bedroom or study, an appropriate room, not a bedroom, make certain it's neat, and dress professionally. Don't interview in your pajamas; your camera may pick up more than you think.

Keep Your Answers Short and Crisp

This advice applies to any interview. No one likes to hear another person drone on and on. If you speak over a minute, you are going into dangerous territory. Likewise, don't give answers that are too short. Terseness is likely to give the impression that you are bored, don't have a full grasp of the questions, or are unable to make conversation—all bad things.

Take Two if You Can

Some of these platforms allow you a second chance. Take it if you feel you can do better.

Prepare for an Automated Telephone Interview

In this scenario, you will probably receive an e-mail with a phone number and codes. You will hear an automated introduction and set of questions. Here, your voice must carry your approach.

Live Interviewing by Telephone

These days, it is common for an interviewer to want to conduct a first-round interview by telephone. If that happens to you, keep these tips in mind.

Stand When You Take the Call

You want to impress any interviewer with your energy and enthusiasm. If you sit and get too relaxed, you won't feel energized. On the other hand, if you stand and move around, you will get the blood flowing and feel engaged.

Smile

Your smile can be *seen* by the person on the other end of the line. Think about a time when you spoke with a friend or loved one on the phone and you felt their emotion. The same applies here. If you are bored or otherwise bothered, the interviewer knows.

Gesture

Everyone gestures, even people who have been blind since birth[3]. Don't think that because no one is watching that they won't sense your gestures. Animate yourself. We want to hire happy, energetic, well-adjusted people, people who smile and gesture. Use the speaker function on your phone to be hands-free. However, test how that sounds with a friend first. Using the speaker function on your phone can sound tinny depending on the acoustics of your home.

Most Importantly, Use Your Voice

Need we say that your voice will carry your personality, sincerity, energy, enthusiasm, and all your other personality traits critical to a telephone interview? Vary your vocal quality. Use the full range of volume in an appropriate way. Use a lower pitch and a slow rate of speed when you're talking. But, as said before, use a higher pitch and faster rate when you want the person on the other end of your call to feel your excitement. Don't exaggerate your speech; just think of having a conversation with a friend, practice with a friend.

---

[3] https://thecut.com/2016/09/blind-people-gesture-like-sighted-people.html

PART IX

Should I Send a "Thank You Letter" After the Interview?

When I was interviewing people, I noted a national epidemic of Thank You letters. Career counselors tell students to send these letters. I can't tell you how many I received and how many I tossed in the trash. I tossed them because I knew they all said the same thing, "Thank you. Give me the job." These students were probably given the template for the same boring message.

Sure, a Thank You is a nice gesture, but it's totally useless, unless it disrupts me. It must do something to differentiate itself from all the same letters. I tell my students not to bother with a Thank You letter, unless they can do something useful with it, that is, they might share an article with me about the industry or perhaps something discussed in the interview. This article must be something, which they believe I have not read and which interests me.

If they feel compelled to send a Thank You letter, they should send something beyond their regards and their hopes that I will hire them. If you feel compelled to send a letter after your interview, be creative. Be different. Be remembered!

I once interviewed candidates for a news media coordinator position at an organization. The choice came down to two people. They qualified equally weighted over all factors, and I was having a hard time deciding whom to choose. Until, one of them sent me, not a Thank You note, but a news release announcing that she had been hired by me. I chose her and she did a great job! As Monster.com said,

"Showing your gratitude is always a good look, especially during a job search. This means promptly thanking your interviewers. A thank-you email after an interview is the most popular—and accepted—method of following up with your potential future employers. Too bad three out of four job seekers don't even bother sending a thank-you, according to an Accountemps survey of human resources (HR) managers." The survey found that only 24 percent of HR managers receive Thank You notes from applicants. However, 80 percent of HR managers say Thank You notes are helpful when reviewing candidates.

"Whether it's a physical letter or an email, this token of appreciation could actually determine if you get the job. "Sending a well-crafted and timely thank-you letter after an interview can add a positive impression to an already positive connection," says Jennifer McClure, president of Unbridled Talent, a Cincinnati firm specializing in talent acquisition, recruiting, and staff development[1]."

Whether or not you decide to send a Thank You letter, you need to have ended your interview on a positive note. This means you made good eye contact, shook hands, and said something very positive about the company. You might say, "I am really impressed with the organization and with you as one of its staff. I felt welcomed and felt that the time we spent together was valuable to both of us. I can see myself as part of this company. I believe I fit, not just through my skillset, but through a shared philosophy and values. If you need additional information, please contact me at the cell phone number on my resume or through email. I look forward eagerly to hearing from you. Thank you."

---

[1]   https://monster.com/career-advice/article/interview-thank-you-letter-send-or-not

PART X

Use the Answers You Receive for the Best Results

So, you've had the interview. You wore your smart suit and polished shoes, and you studied and answered all the questions you thought you would be asked. You have a great feeling that you will get the offer. Now, slow down. Take a breath and think about things.

I recommend that you should never accept a job just to have a job. Never! I don't care how poor you are, how many student loans or car payments are due, or how bad the economy is. Don't take any old job because someone is willing to hire you! Identify the work you've always wanted to do. Narrow your search of companies that you've always wanted to work for. Learn as much as you can about those companies. Go for a job in one of those companies.

In the process, however, if you learn some things in your research or in the interview that make you suspect of the company, back away, fast!

Suppose you learn that the company uses the Jack Welch *rank and yank* system of employee retention and promotion. You may not feel good about working in an environment that *ranks and yanks*. If so, save yourself some wasted time, heartache, and heartburn and walk away from the job offer.

Suppose you're a woman or member of a minority and you can't find information, either from research or interviews, which suggest an equal opportunity environment.

You scan through pictures of the company's management team, and you see no racial or gender diversity; walk away from that job offer!

If you'd like to spend time away on family leave and your interviewer pooh poohs it, you should walk away from that company. If you're community-minded and the organization with which you're interviewing has no programs for involvement in the local community, walk! If the interviewer can't give a valid reason for the departure of the person who had the job before you, do some searching to find the reason for that person's departure.

If the company is on shaky financial ground, walk away from it. I've done the opposite and lived to regret it.

Conclusion

Sometimes, it seems like finding the right job is an act of providence, best left to chance. It doesn't have to be that way. If you begin by understanding exactly what you want to do with your life and then seek the kind of employment that will allow you to fulfill that desire, you will have saved yourself much time and potentially much heartbreak.

A friend told me she could never work in an office; she eventually became a city detective. Know the environment you will feel most comfortable in and make your career decisions develop from there.

If you spend as much as half of your life doing something that you dislike, you will be unhappy, and your employer will be unhappy as well. Spend some time in contemplation. Know as much about yourself as possible and then learn as much as possible about your potential employer. More than anything, learn as much about the person who will supervise you and the people with whom you will work every day. Many studies have proven that people leave jobs because they don't get along with their supervisor. Ask questions about these people; be proactive. Remember, you are bringing your skills and talents to them. Without the best employees, companies consist only of empty buildings. Take some control; it's a dynamic process.

About the Author

Edward Barr has taught thousands of people over a 25-year career at Carnegie Mellon University (CMU) in Pittsburgh, PA, USA, where he currently teaches and coaches computational finance majors to communicate better when they take jobs on Wall Street.

Before beginning his career at CMU, he served as a marketing executive in both for-profit and not-for-profit companies for over 20 years, including Chief Marketing Officer at iCarnegie, a CMU for-profit. As a marketing professional, he conducted business in Brazil, Colombia, China, India, and the United States and has served as a freelance writer and marketing consultant for marketing firms.

He has taught in China, India, Amsterdam, London, Kazakhstan, Mexico, and Panama. He has taught corporate executives and staff at Cognizant, an American IT service company with over 200,000 employees in the United States and across the globe.

While at CMU, he has also taught professional writing, business communication, marketing, negotiation, and strategy.

Index

OTHER TITLES IN THE BUSINESS CAREER DEVELOPMENT COLLECTION

Vilma Barr, Consultant, Editor

- *Rules Don't Work for Me* by Gail Summers
- *Fast Forward Your Career* by Simonetta Lureti and Lucio Furlani
- *100 Skills of the Successful Sales Professional* by Alex Dripchak
- *Negotiate Your Way to Success* by Kasia Jagodzinska
- *Personal and Career Development* by Claudio A. Rivera and Elza Priede
- *Getting It Right When It Matters Most* by Tony Gambill and Scott Carbonara
- *How to Make Good Business Decisions* by J.C. Baker
- *The Power of Belonging* by Sunita Sehmi
- *Your GPS to Employment Success* by Beverly A. Williams
- *Emotional Intelligence at Work* by Richard M. Contino and Penelope J. Holt
- *The Champion Edge* by Alan R. Zimmerman
- *Shaping Your Future* by Rita Rocker-Craft
- *Finding Your Career Niche* by Anne S. Klein
- *The Trust Factor* by Russell von Frank
- *Creating A Business and Personal Legacy* by J. Mark Munoz

Concise and Applied Business Books

The Collection listed above is one of 30 business subject collections that Business Expert Press has grown to make BEP a premiere publisher of print and digital books. Our concise and applied books are for...

- Professionals and Practitioners
- Faculty who adopt our books for courses
- Librarians who know that BEP's Digital Libraries are a unique way to offer students ebooks to download, not restricted with any digital rights management
- Executive Training Course Leaders
- Business Seminar Organizers

Business Expert Press books are for anyone who needs to dig deeper on business ideas, goals, and solutions to everyday problems. Whether one print book, one ebook, or buying a digital library of 110 ebooks, we remain the affordable and smart way to be business smart. For more information, please visit www.businessexpertpress.com, or contact sales@businessexpertpress.com.

CPSIA information can be obtained
at www.ICGtesting.com
Printed in the USA
BVHW051412210821
614355BV00008B/206